Endorsem
The Entrepreneurial Compass

"At a time in our evolution when we are asked to be connected to one device or another, choose to sit with *The Entrepreneurial Compass*, and you'll be rewarded with new ideas for self-care and reminders of how important it is to pause to reach our goals. Laura's years of experience shine through her new book guiding a path towards success while simultaneously leading us back to ourselves. A must-read for anyone seeking the work-life balance." – Rachel Hogancamp, Managing Partner, Rasa Spa, www.rasaspa.com

"*The Entrepreneurial Compass* is a remarkable book that helps guide readers to embrace and live out the mindful practices necessary for upgrading success. The integrative approach of business wisdom, practices, and real authentic research creates a solid structure to apply to every success model. It's a powerful read with great exercises to advance your business." - Dr. Pam Denton, Intuitive Enterprises, LLC and Vision Pro Business consultant,www.pamdenton.com

"Laura's insight into the world of entrepreneurship is a no-nonsense approach for success. To live your divine purpose with a true roadmap for daily reflection, living with joy, and giving back with an open heart. That for me is truly living an abundant life." - Bonita Shear, Kundalini Yoga instructor, and owner of "Happiness is my Birthright," www.bonitaim.com

"YES! Yes! Yes! Laura's words strike a deep chord within me. Yes... This is who I am. Yes... This is who I dream to be. Yes... This is how I get there. *The Entrepreneurial Compass* is an elevated companion on the path to self-discovery and self-mastery. Thank you, Laura, for sharing your creative spark so eloquently and inspiring me to remember and explore mine." – Alicia Mooney, mom, massage therapist, retreat leader and creativity coach, A Centered Self, www.acenteredself.com

"The Entrepreneurial Compass is a fun read for anyone who has the desire to become or is an Entrepreneur. Many of the shared stories in the book are inspirational and also remind you to use your inner compass to return to yourself. At the end of the day, enjoy what you do." – Michael Prego, owner, Empire Mechanical

"As a fellow entrepreneur, I appreciate Laura's desire to share nuggets of inspiration and gentle guidance to self-discovery, so that we might all expand to our fullest potential, as well as, support one another in attaining theirs. Knowing Laura on a personal level, I can say that she is what she professes...just being in her presence inspires and uplifts those around her, myself included. Her beautiful soul and wisdom shine through this book, ready to be amplified throughout each of us as we collectively touch the world." – Mariesa Dranschak, certified conscious life coach and teacher, www.myconsciouslifecoach.com

"Laura's way with words coupled with her tremendous insight and experience make this book a must read for any entrepreneur! She convinces us to believe that we are the creators of our destiny and dreaming big is essential to our success. The inspirational quotes and ponder questions challenge the reader to slow down and think about what they really want. If you're looking for motivation to be your best self, Laura's book will be transformational!" – Deborah J. Cabral, author, TV host, founder, The DeClutter Coach, and DC Efficiency Consulting, www.decluttercoachdeb.com, www.dceffconsult.com

"Through *The Entrepreneurial Compass*, Laura Ponticello validates, encourages and guides you to embrace the creative entrepreneur within you and claim the new paradigm of business for your company." – Sheila Applegate, bestselling author, transformational life coach and founder of Consciously Awesome, www.sheilaapplegate.com

"Laura Ponticello's opening quote by Sheryl Sandburg, "If you're offered a seat on a rocket ship, don't ask what seat. Just get on," is a metaphor for the treasure of her third book, *The Entrepreneurial Compass*. Ponticello offers us not only a compass but a detailed roadmap, to both internal, as well as, external success. Combining practical suggestions with her advanced spiritual knowledge of the power of thoughts, words, intentions, and affirmations, *The Entrepreneurial Compass* is a must-read for anyone hoping to make their dreams come true." – Traci Medford-Rosow, award-winning USA Today bestselling author of *UNBLINDED*, www.tracimedfordrosow.com

The Entrepreneurial Compass

A GUIDE TO JOY, PROSPERITY AND A LIFE IN BALANCE

Laura Ponticello

Divine Phoenix Books
Skaneateles, New York

Laura Ponticello/Divine Phoenix Books, LLC. Publishing Company, PO Box 1001, Skaneateles, New York 13152
www.lauraponticello.com, www.divinephoenixbooks.com

Book layout, www.bookdesigntemplates.com ©2017
Book cover design: Christopher Moebs
Source quotes: www.brainyquote.com, www.goodreads.com, www.wikipedia.com
Photos: © 2018 www.dreamstime.com
Author photo: Laure Lillie Photography
Individuals may order books, and special discounts are available on a minimum quantity purchases made by corporations, associations, and others. For details, contact the "Special Sales Department" at the mailing address above.
The Entrepreneurial Compass/Laura Ponticello. —1st edition
ISBN 9781791982003

Foreword

"In her latest book, *The Entrepreneurial Compass,* award-winning and best-selling author Laura Ponticello distills decades of hands-on entrepreneurial experience, and thousands of hours of empirical research, into a timely and vibrant manifesto for achieving one's dreams. *The Entrepreneurial Compass* reminds us to take pause, reflect, and rejoice in all of life's lessons. Further, Laura Ponticello's unique perspective provides the reader with the tools to decode limiting beliefs and behaviors, while realigning one's focus and energy through inspired choices and purposeful action.

Life is a journey. *The Entrepreneurial Compass* is a must-read for anyone seeking to ignite their creative energy to think and dream big, visualize positive outcomes, and actualize their destiny."

Mark C. Coleman, husband, father, advisor, best-selling and award-winning author of *The Sustainability Generation: The Politics of Change and Why Personal Accountability is Essential NOW!* and *Time To Trust: Mobilizing Humanity for a Sustainable Future,* **www.timetotrustbook.com**

Dedication

To mom, dad and sister for being a
steadfast cheering squad over the years.

Thank you. ♥

"You're off to great places!

Today is your day!

Your mountain is waiting, so...

get on your way."

— Dr. Seuss

PREFACE

Welcome and Note to Reader

"The world is a possibility, if only you will discover it." —Ralph Ellison

Welcome to a playground for exploration. How incredible it is to engage you in an adventure to discover, develop and put into practice actions that will amplify the ability for your success. Once you awaken to your magnanimous potential, you will realize that incredible possibilities exist.

As a fellow entrepreneur, I thought it might be nice to come together to reflect and share experiences. Like-wise, to celebrate each other's accomplishments and support our wildest dreams materializing.

As you endeavor ahead, you will have the opportunity to expand your knowledge base. Whether you are a newbie, a seasoned pro or an established professional, you can fine-tune modes of operation, and gain awareness and understanding of behavioral tendencies to achieve optimal performance.

The Entrepreneurial Compass presents life lessons and success stories from entrepreneurs since we tend to learn from each other. Nuggets of inspiration range in topical areas such as; "How I Spend Energy," "Maintaining Work-Life Balance," "Communication Techniques for Positive Customer Engagement," "Creativity as an Amplification Instrument," "Intuition as a Gauge-Point," "Self-Care Practices," "Overcoming Limited Beliefs," "Propelling Power Thoughts," "Leveraging Support Champions," and "Claiming Your Wildest Dream." Also, look for these prompts in the book: "Points to Ponder," "For Reflection," and "Actions to Put into Practice."

Since everyone processes information at a different pace, allocate as much time as you need to absorb the content in this book. Make notes. Turn down pages. Ponder, question, and test practical suggestions.

During the discovery process, you will explore beliefs, thoughts, and ways of operating. **Taking the time** to discover your strengths and focus on perfecting the skills that will help you become the best in your industry becomes a very crucial decision point in every entrepreneur's journey. [1]

As with any new endeavor, be open-minded. Don't be afraid to take chances. Growth is a vital part of the expansion process, and risk and opportunity go hand in hand.

The bottom line is don't limit yourself by thinking small. Dream the wildest dream for yourself!

I look forward to where you go from here in remembering, awakening, and claiming of your complete awesomeness on the entrepreneurial journey.

With ardent support,

Laura

THE UNIVERSE IS CONTINUALLY
SUPPORTING YOU.
YOU CAN INFLUENCE YOUR REALITY!
WHAT YOU THINK, AND FEEL MATTERS
GIVEN THERE IS AN ENERGY THAT
MAGNIFIES AS YOU ALIGN WITH LIFE'S
PURPOSE AND CLAIM THE TOTALITY OF
YOUR POTENTIAL.

"Once you make a decision,

the universe conspires to make it happen."

— *RALPH WALDO EMERSON*

MIGHT BE HELPFUL ON THE EXPLORATION JOURNEY

"If you are offered a seat on the rocket ship,
don't ask what seat. Just get on."
—Sheryl Sandburg

You should equip yourself with success tools. As you venture forward, it may be wise to acquire the following: an exploration notebook, a water bottle, and a quote or visual image that inspires/motivates you.

- Notebook – please label it, "Exploration Journey." You can utilize the notes section of a cellular phone and computer too. The notes area serves as a place for you to write down your thoughts. Reflective spaces are essential spots to pen ideas, review progress and get in touch with your feelings.

- Water bottle – we forget to hydrate ourselves when we are busy. Water fuels the brain and stimulates blood flow. You need brain energy to do your job.

- Motivational reminders – as the book, *Ten Ways to Stay Motivated as an Entrepreneur* conveys, the key to staying motivated as an entrepreneur is remembering why you embarked on your journey in the first place.

  Locate a quote that speaks to you. Download it, frame it and use it as a motivation tool. Place a visual reminder on your desk, cellular phone or inside your exploration notebook of what motivates you to work. For example, you might choose a picture of your family, or of a vacation destination, you dream of visiting in the future.

As you move through your day, take time to reboot and recharge. You are encouraged to allocate fifteen minutes for a re-energizing break. During this time, stretch, walk or move around. Fresh air is also super healthy, so, open a window or step outside into nature.

The Significance of the Compass

"When you follow a star, you know you will never reach that star; rather it will guide you to where you want to go, so it is with the world. It will only ever lead you back to yourself." — Jeanette Winterson

Throughout history, sailors have utilized a compass as an instrument for guidance. Cardinal points (north, south, east, and west) gauge the direction. The significance of the "compass" as a symbol within this book is to remind you that directional instruments exist to help get you back on track.

One modern-day example is a hand-held GPS (Global Positioning System). This device guides those moving towards a destination point. A person can venture out into the wilderness, for example, and this tool will help navigate a path forward. Because there are times when one can become lost, the GPS can also help a person return to the path that will lead to their final destination.

Recently, during a women's outdoors sportsman day, I tried a recreational activity called Orienteering. In Orienteering, participants use a map and compass to navigate towards checkpoints along an unfamiliar course.[2]

While in the woods, I found myself wandering aimlessly throughout the terrain and needed geographical insight to resume my path. Therefore, the compass served as a directional tool. Since the human brain can only hold so much information, it comes as a relief that there are devices to help with such tasks as finding the best route. [3]

During this experience, I had a reflective thought that entrepreneurs might find themselves veering off course and need of a way to re-route themselves. We don't intend to get off track, but it happens. Because entrepreneurs need clarity of direction, a compass is an excellent instrument to utilize.

The New England Orienteering Club has this to say about staying on track, "You know those days where it feels like your feet barely touch the ground as you run? Where the navigation comes so easily that every feature appears in front of you at exactly the right time? Those are good days. Unfortunately, it's pretty rare that everything lines up exactly as it should, so those good days are few and far between. What can you do when those days happen?"[4]

While mechanical devices such as the hand-held GPS are terrific navigational tools; one of the most significant tools available is your inner guidance system; the compass within you!

In "Accessing Your Inner Guidance," professional development expert Brian Tracy imparts "The wonderful thing is you're constructed so that if you simply listen carefully to yourself - to your mind, your body and your emotions, and follow the guidance you're given, you can dramatically enhance the quality of your life."[5]

Ultimately, the compass serves as a support mechanism to guide you. By tapping into your inner compass, you naturally align your passion and purpose to move towards the work that you enjoy.[6]

This book will help to activate the compass within you. It will engage the part of you that makes business decisions and personal choices, and that ultimately aspires to live a life of balance, joy, and prosperity.

Contributing writer Sherri Campbell offers insight in "Seven Ways Entrepreneurs Can Master Self Awareness" about retrieving your inner guidance. "The first steps toward true success are always inward. Successful entrepreneurs know how to master who they are and harness their inner power, instincts, and intuition. Knowing themselves with clarity leads them to the right deals and business ventures. If they do not have acute self-awareness, they will come up against the counterforce of out-of-control emotions, leading to their downfall. With self-awareness, it's possible to predict the power relationships necessary for success better."[7]

"Your inner knowing

is your only true compass."

— *JOY PAGE*

CHAPTER ONE

Introduction

"Twenty years from now you will be more disappointed by the things that you didn't do than by the ones you did do. So, throw off the bowlines. Sail away from the safe harbor. Catch the trade winds in your sails. Explore. Dream. Discover."— Mark Twain

I have twenty years of experience as a coach, entrepreneur, and teacher in the area of personal transformation. I understand the challenges of managing a business, and the demands of meeting customer expectations while attempting to be innovative. Additionally, I am familiar with the juggernaut that is striving for work-life balance while longing to live a purposeful life.

As a result of coaching entrepreneurs and leaders over the years, I have found character trait commonalities. A desire for respect and appreciation exists because of the work performed. Eight-five percent of the professionals I interviewed for this book, share an internal conflict over a deep-seated desire to be: "all things to all people." This desire stems from the mindset that entrepreneurs must wear multiple hats. Entrepreneurs can burn out and develop frustration due to constant demands.

Many entrepreneurs commented, "I'm at crossroads of how to scale the business to the next level while obtaining time for myself or my family." Additionally, several entrepreneurs noted, "I have many ideas; however, I need clarity of direction to use my skills the best way I can."

WHY ENTREPRENEURS START A BUSINESS

Why you start a company influences how you operate today. It is important to remind yourself of the passion that you hold for your business and what motivates you to go to work. There are several reasons an entrepreneur may start a business:

- A longing for more freedom and flexibility than a traditional job provides.
- A problem occurs, and a solution to the problem is offered through the creation of a product, company or organization.
- A need to honor a calling or passion towards a life skill.

- The family-owned business exists, and there is a desire to join the company and eventually take over the business.

WHAT MOTIVATES YOU?

WHAT MOTIVATES YOU TO SHOW UP FOR WORK?

YOUR TIME IS VALUABLE

An entrepreneur's most valuable resource is time because once it is gone, it does not come back. As author David Hieatt expresses in his book, *Why Brands with Purpose Do Better and Matter More*, "Each day you're given 86,400 seconds from the 'Time Bank.' Everyone is given the same. There are no exceptions. Once you make your withdrawal, you're free to spend it as you want. The 'Time Bank' won't tell you how to spend it. Time poorly spent will not be replaced with more time. Time doesn't do refunds."[8]

Richard Branson, thought leader and founder of Virgin Atlantic, imparts "I'm going to keep this short and simple. The way in which you look at the time, and the way that you choose to invest it, will be the ultimate factor determining your success as an entrepreneur."[9]

HOW DO YOU SPEND YOUR TIME?

A healthy state of being will benefit your ability to run a company or organization. Do you take time to be the healthiest version of you?

You may be performing functions that are not critical to your job, and there may be duties, you can eliminate. Therefore, please review how you exude time in a day and where you place your attention. As you consider how you spend your time, is there anything you can delegate or eliminate? Once you review how you spend your time, you can shift energy towards the tasks that yield the most productive outcome, instead of being weighed down by things you don't enjoy.

PLEASE COMPLETE THIS SENTENCE:

I DESIRE MORE MOMENTS TO...

IN THINKING ABOUT TIME, THE QUESTION BECOMES, "HOW WILL YOU ALLOCATE YOUR TIME WISELY?"

CHAPTER TWO

The Greatest Asset is You

"Investing in yourself is just as important –
if not more important than investing in
your business." — Emily Thompson

While speaking with over one hundred entrepreneurs and organizational leaders at the "Lakewood Women Connecting Women" event in Ohio, I learned firsthand what motivates entrepreneurs to start a business. As well, I came to understand the daily challenges facing entrepreneurs, such as: maintaining a work-life balance, carving out self-care time, meeting increasing customer demands while growing revenue and the need for capital investment to scale the business to next level.

THE SEARCH FOR A LIFE IN BALANCE

"Self-care is never a selfish act; it is simply good stewardship of the only gift I have, the gift I was put on earth to offer to others."
— Parker Palmer

THE FUNDAMENTAL QUESTION THAT KEEPS COMING UP IN MULTIPLE DIALOGUES IS "HOW DO I ACHIEVE A LIFE IN BALANCE?"

Barb, a veteran entrepreneur, communicates, "Once you lose a semblance of yourself by operating from a space of constantly doing, you forgo the essence of who you are. As a result, the business and family life suffer since you aren't truly present in any environment. If you don't make time for yourself, everything will burn and crash around you. As a consequence, you will be like a riverbed depleted of the water required to sustain the flow of the river."

I WISH I HAD MORE TIME

In speaking to entrepreneurs, I discovered that a common frustration is the giving away of energy too freely to everyday jobs that are not enjoyable!

LEARN TO SAY NO

"Learn to say 'no' to the good so you can say 'yes' to the best." —John C. Maxwell

Entrepreneur and *Shark Tank* television star Mark Cuban said, "Every no gets me closer to a Yes!"

As you say no to those things that you don't want to do or that are utterly unnecessary, you free yourself. In "Three Must-Have Scripts for Saying No to Clients Nicely," Melody Wilding shares, "Saying no is a gift you give yourself! Not only does it help reduce calendar chaos and anxiety, but it also makes you available both physically and mentally for the things that are vital to your business. This action serves almost like business armor, protecting your bottom line and your most important resource: time."[10]

As I think about how I spend my time, I recognize there are tasks which I perform that no longer serve me. I review my daily calendar and label functions as 1. Not essential to running a business, 2. Necessary to run a business, 3. Tasks that can be done once a week or monthly (payroll, invoicing, etc.), 4. Self-care time.

Once I shed the tasks marked as "not essential," I can allocate time to take a yoga class, meditate, vision planning time, or creative time.

POINT TO PONDER

WHAT DO YOU NEED TO STOP DOING AND START DOING INSTEAD?

ENTREPRENEURIAL TIP

Automation leads to greater efficiency of workflow. Automate as much as possible. The average employee spends twenty-eight percent of their workday, reading and answering email, according to a study by management consulting firm McKinsey and Company. Keeping emails brief and to the point can help you reclaim some of this time. [11]

DON'T HAVE ANY REGRETS

In summary, "No one lies on their deathbed wishing he (she) had time to reply to one more email, but a great many people express regrets about not having treated life with more purpose." —Todd Henry

CHAPTER THREE

Take Time to Dream

"If you can dream it, you can do it."
—Walt Disney

As you reclaim energy, you may feel a renewed sense of excitement. This will allow you to choose where you place your attention and how to spend time. You are free to explore other ideas, try new activities, and spend time daydreaming. Furthermore, you can permit yourself to dream about your vision for yourself and the business.

Freelance writer, Vivian Nunez conveys the positive benefit of taking time to dream. "Part of the bad reputation comes from the notion that dreams never lead to action, as an entrepreneur, I can say with confidence that I wouldn't be where I am if it weren't for the moments I claimed as my time to dream. They didn't have to be impressively great dreams; honestly most times they weren't even close to feasible, but the fringe benefits were indisputable."[12]

Vivan continues, "The time I gave myself to dream was synonymous with the time that I didn't judge my ideas and just let the creativity happen."[13]

WHY DREAMING CAN HELP YOU

In "Why Dreaming is so Important for Entrepreneurs," CEO Richard Branson shares, "Dreaming is one of humanity's greatest gifts. It champions aspiration, spurs innovation, leads to change and propels us forward. In a world without dreams, there would be no adventure, no moon landing, no female CEOs, no civil rights. What a half-lived and tragic existence we would have. We should all dream big, and encourage others to do so, too."[14]

The Associated Press published an interesting piece on J.K. Rowling, the New York Times bestselling author of *Harry Potter.* Rowling dreamed that she was the boy wizard as she wrote the seven-book series' final installment — work she claimed had left her feeling both "elated and overwrought." Rowling has noted on her official website that when working hard at writing scenes, some have been planned more than twelve years ago. [15]

REACH FOR THE STARS

"Every great dream begins with a dreamer. Always remember, you have within you the strength, the patience, and the passion to reach for the stars to change the world." — Harriet Tubman

In a dream state, you allow for an idea to unfold in your imagination. You envision something in the future. In the spirit of thinking beyond the current moment, I invite you to meet a dream of yours. Examples of possible dreams could be a future family vacation or a personal wish, like climbing the Adirondack High Peaks. Maybe you want to open a bakery, take a cruise on the Nile River, or roll out a technology app you've been designing for years.

FOR REFLECTION – PLEASE COMPLETE THESE SENTENCES

MY DREAM FOR THE BUSINESS IS…

IN MY LIFE, I DESIRE MORE OF…

THE DREAM BOARD

"The entrepreneur is essentially a visualizer and actualizer. He can visualize something, and when he visualizes it, he sees exactly how to make it happen."
—Robert L. Schwartz

In my line of work, I interface with many different personality types. Joe was a client of mine. His hairline was balding, and he had a jolly laugh. His professional field was technology. Some of his colleagues, especially those on the executive team, thought Joe was out of his mind since he tended to daydream a lot. Most of his dream time included thoughts about future events that he conjured before they transpired.

On a daily basis, Joe took periods to close his eyes. In this state, he imagined the future. On the whiteboard in his office, which was kept open for staff to witness, Joe posted diagrams, pictures, and expressions that depicted his futurist visions. He created a pictorial of what he saw in his mind.

Joe labeled the whiteboard, "THE DREAM BOARD!"

One day, Joe sat me down alongside the whiteboard, and commented, "Laura, don't ever limit yourself! Aren't we capable of dreaming about future possibilities? I say let's take everyone in the department somewhere fun in the country and have the time of our lives to celebrate technological developments when we meet our goals." Then Joe opened his dream board and showcased his vision.

Within thirteen months, his entire staff was in Beverly Hills, California (including me). A fun celebration took place. First, the team played a game of scavenger hunt in the Ripley museum. Later, the team went to the Beverly Hills Wilshire Hotel for a dinner event.

From the podium in the front of the room, Joe grabbed the microphone and shared, "We did it. I dreamed this up because I knew that we could do anything we dreamed about. That is what we do, create ideas and turn them into realities." Joe's team was responsible for new technology developments, and the implementation of a global purchasing software earmarked to save the company a substantial amount of money due to the automation of functions for employees and vendors.

What is fascinating about future dreaming, in this case, is the level of detail that Joe envisioned in advance of the dream becoming real. He saw the evening as it would unfold. He described in detail on his dream board, the sights, and smells of the event as if he was already there.

As Gloria Steinem noted, "Dreaming, after all, is a form of planning." [16]

POINT TO PONDER

DO YOU TAKE TIME TO DREAM?

DO YOU ENCOURAGE YOUR KIDS, STAFF, AND COWORKERS TO SPEND TIME DREAMING?

Best You Magazine, a leading personal and professional growth publication featured "Sixteen Reasons Why It's So Important to Follow Your Dreams." In this article, contributing writer Joel Brown conveyed "Your dreams have no limits; you are the creator of your dreams, big or small. When this is understood, you are able to design a way to favor your plan and accomplish your end goal. So, don't let the dreams within you die."[17]

CHAPTER FOUR

Leapfrog – The Door of Opportunity

"Every time you state what you want or believe, you're the first to hear it. It's a message to both you and others about what you think is possible. Don't put a ceiling on yourself." — Oprah Winfrey

Our nature as humans is to desire expansion. Ultimately, we don't want to remain stationary. The temperaments of seeking and striving to exist pushes us beyond the boundaries of comfort. One critical element to growth taking place is the willingness to try! Growth requires stepping outside of comfort zones.

One common trait among entrepreneurs is that they don't want to grow old and regret not taking chances. This desire is what drives them to do all that they can across a lifetime, and if they end up failing, they know they will have learned some lesson; they will have gained practical experience and the ability to tackle similar situations will come easily in the future.[18]

TRANSFORMING FEAR INTO VISION

American journalist Soledad Obrien speaks of fear in this way; "I've learned that fear limits you and your vision. It serves as a blinder to what may be just a few steps down the road for you. The journey is valuable but believing in your talents, your abilities, and your self-worth can permit you to walk down an even brighter path. Transforming fear into freedom - how great is that?"[19]

I remember watching a movie on *Lifetime* television network, "Coco Chanel," about a French fashion designer and businesswoman, Gabrielle Bonheur Chanel. The film was captivating for many reasons, mostly its portrayal of a woman who defied the odds and built a successful business. Coco sacrificed a lot to be an innovator in the fashion industry.

Coco originated from modest roots and grew up in an orphanage run by nuns. They taught her how to sew, and this skill set became instrumental in her future as a fashion designer.

Coco began her career selling hats that she designed in a Paris storefront. Despite the naysayers who questioned her ability to sell different hats, she attained success. This accomplishment gave her the courage to continue to take risks as a businesswoman.

Her first taste of clothing success emerged from designing a dress out of an old jersey on a chilly day. Later in her career, Coco conquered another feat that proved to be a fruitful venture. She struck a deal with a partner to help manufacture CHANEL No. 5 perfume. The fragrance became a highly regarded product. To this day, the scent is world-renowned.

Coco's life story resonated for many reasons. Coco was fearless. She was willing to do what was necessary to build a brand in the marketplace. She saw a future for herself beyond the current moment, and she anticipated many possibilities for growth. Without failure, Coco wouldn't have achieved success. Coco trusted herself even when no one else did. She epitomized tenacity which is an entrepreneurial asset.

The Australian Institute of Business stated in "Five Reasons Why Entrepreneurs Take Risks," that "You'll never know until you try. For the majority of entrepreneurs, a chance is a case of 'what if' and is seen as a means of advancing their business in some way. No matter how calculated it is, you can never be sure that risk will pay off. There is only one way to find out."[20]

As Frederick Wilcox said, "Progress always involves risks. You can't steal second base and keep your foot on first." [21]

FOR REFLECTION

ARE THERE AREAS OF YOUR LIFE IN WHICH YOU ARE AFRAID TO TAKE A RISK?

WHAT CAN YOU DO TO OVERCOME ANY FEAR OF THE UNKNOWN?

LESSONS FROM ENTREPRENEURS ON TAKING CHANCES

"When one door of happiness closes, another opens, but often we look so long at the closed door that we do not see the one that has been opened for us."
—Helen Keller

"I knew that when I was eighty, I was not going to regret having tried...I knew that if I failed, I wouldn't regret that. I knew the one thing I might regret is not ever having tried, and I knew that would haunt me every day"[22], says Jeff Bezos, CEO of Amazon.

Bonita, a successful wellness entrepreneur, and yoga teacher expressed during a workshop that I attended, "Every time an opportunity arrives, I recognize that fear of the unknown can hold me back or thrust me ahead. I have two choices: walk through a golden door of the possibility and take a risk or run in the opposite direction, out of fear."

"I realize that leaping through the golden door of opportunity is incredibly rewarding!" — Bonita.

Bonita drank a sip of tea and continued, "During periods of doubt, mental tapes that self-sabotage the psyche with negative thoughts can limit me to think small. I learned how to adjust the recording in the mind when negative chatter ramps up. I say "cancel" when a negative thought emerges and instead, focus on a positive thought."

Point to Ponder - Be mindful of what you play out in your mind! It will make a huge difference in your life.

In the article "My Contributions To Entrepreneurship Theory," economist Professor G. Klein suggests that if you think an opportunity doesn't exist, create the opportunity. "The entrepreneur does not know in advance whether the action will be successful. But they do expect that they, as individuals, have the wherewithal and the capacity to bring their imagined future state to reality. They act under conditions of uncertainty. They create new firms, new products, new services, and new markets under conditions of uncertainty something that people without entrepreneurial grit would not tackle."[23]

CHAPTER FIVE

Break Free of Limitations

"It's your road and your road alone. Others may walk it with you, but no one can walk it for you." — Rumi

On this rollercoaster ride of life, you see, feel and experience a multitude of emotions. Occurrences with others are perceived as positive or negative. Encounters with employees, customers, vendors or even family members are considered to be good or bad. We label each other based on our interactions and evaluate an individual's performance on specific criteria or prejudgments.

When you stop judging others, you can let go of self-judgment too. You can permit yourself to release outdated beliefs. Then, you can invite in original ways of thinking.

LETTING GO OF LIMITED BELIEFS

Often, a limited belief is tied to fear. Limited beliefs may stem from inquiries such as: "What if I fail? How can I do this? What if things don't work out for me? Will I be successful?" And the list goes on. In the midst of these moments of uncertainty recall that courage lives within you. You are only as limited as you believe yourself to be. And you can step over and walk through any limitations to open new doors of opportunities.

Coach and author Mike DiLeone writes in "How to Let Go of Negative Limiting Beliefs About Yourself" that "Changing behavior need not be intimidating. It requires that you be mindful when making decisions. You'll want to make decisions that will get you to where you want to go in life. I ask myself a single game-changing question in everything I do, *is this in alignment with my authentic purpose?* If it isn't, I choose instead to do something that is."[24]

The following example showcases what happens when you experience a change of circumstance and how you can muster the courage to break free of limitations. Included after that is another case example where limited belief holds back a person back from expanding their skills.

Mom was an office manager at her brother's dental practice. Her job entailed billing, event coordination, scheduling, and customer interaction. She witnessed her brother 's success as an entrepreneur and attributed it to his willingness to adapt and change with the times. Another asset to his success was his desire to perfect his craft by taking classes; he became an expert in his industry.

After thirty years of working for her brother's practice, Mom retired. She decided to take energy healing classes as a means to help others. One year later, Mom was diagnosed with breast cancer. After successful medical treatment, Mom wanted to encourage other cancer survivors. She pursued and received a grant to work with breast cancer patients.

FOLLOW YOUR ASPIRATIONS

Along the path of change, Mom questioned herself. She wrestled with questions like "Am I capable of learning a new skill? Do I have what it takes to succeed?" Mom conquered doubts. She kept working towards her goal. For the final step in her Reiki training, Mom invited me to join her in Glen Falls, New York where she studied with international leader, William Rand, who presented her with a Master in Reiki certificate.

Mom and me celebrating her achievement.

RESISTANCE CAN HOLD YOU BACK

"Either push your limits or suffocate in your comfort zone." — Arun Purang

Sue was an executive assistant to my boss. She was efficient and an organizer of people. Sue resisted change; specifically, anything to do with technological advancements. Additionally, she liked to do things her way.

An international company acquired our work company. As a result, it was necessary to use software to connect with employees in various international offices. Sue had to comply and start to use an e-calendar system and an electronic global invoice system. Both software interfaces required her to learn new technological skills.

Sue was fearful of the unfamiliar. She dug her heels in and bucked at the opportunity to acquire a new skill set. Although numerous classes offered training on the latest technological system, Sue reverted into her old ways of doing things. I tried to convince Sue that she could expand her knowledge base and skill set to be more marketable.

The bottom line is Sue struggled with change. As a result, the company was forced to eliminate Sue because she refused to use the new technological system. Sue had a hard time acquiring another job because many companies required technical software proficiency in an executive assistant.

FOR REFLECTION

ARE YOU OPEN TO CHANGE OR DO YOU RESIST IT?

STEP OUTSIDE YOUR COMFORT ZONE

"Sometimes we have to step out of our comfort zones. We have to break the rules. And we have to discover the sensuality of fear. We need to face it, challenge it, dance with it." — Kyra Davis

Professor Andy Molinsky of management and psychology at Brandeis University highlights in "Why Stepping Outside Your Comfort Zone is the Key to Being a Successful Entrepreneur" to review what's holding you back. "Take an inventory of your excuses and ask yourself if they are truly legitimate. If someone else offered you those same excuses, would you see them as legitimate reasons for them to decline?"[25]

Stef Crowder, business coach and podcast host talks with business owners about overcoming uncomfortable challenges in their business on her podcast "Courage and Clarity," www.courageandclarity.com/podcast. She advises "You've got to have the courage to see your vision come true. If you stick with it, you'll be rewarded for your conviction and your steady action towards your dream."

CHAPTER SIX

Kicking Fear to the Curb

"Only those who will risk going too far can possibly find out how far it is possible to go." — T. S. Eliot

Being an individual who is fearless isn't easy. Camille Preston, Founder and CEO of Aim Leadership says in "Why Fear Makes You a Better Leader" that "When we act in the face of adversity, when we move toward something that scares the living daylights out of us, when we move out of our comfort zone and past our terror's edge, we can grow and develop in ways we never imagined." [26]

HOW DO YOU MAKE A SHIFT TOWARDS EMPOWERMENT?

Empowerment is the power, right or authority to do something. As an entrepreneur, you will need to stand tall in owning why your company's product or services are a benefit for others, as well as in who you are and what talents you offer to the world. To be successful, you will need to live from an empowered state. Entrepreneurs need to act instead of waiting around for someone else to get things done.

FROM "10 THINGS YOU CAN DO TO BOOST YOUR CONFIDENCE:"

"The best way to overcome fear is to face it head-on. By doing something that scares you every day and gaining confidence from every experience, you will see your self-confidence soar. So, get out of your comfort zone and face your fears!"[27]

ULTIMATELY THE BUCK STARTS WITH YOU!

"Don't let others tell you what you can't do. Don't let the limitations of others limit your vision. If you can remove your self-doubt and believe in yourself, you can achieve what you never thought possible." — Roy T. Bennett, author, *The Light in the Heart*

If you don't believe in you, who will? A big misnomer exists that "tooting one's own horn" is self-serving. But if you don't tell people about your products or services, how can prospective customers know what you have to offer? One straightforward way to make a shift away from the self-serving mindset is to share why you started your company. Tell a prospective client or vendor what the intention is for a product or service. Be enthusiastic about sharing your story and the company's mission! You might be pleasantly surprised by the great response. Remarkable things can happen when you own and actively express the power of your story and your company mission.

Author Zech Newman notes in the online article, "Five Roadblocks that Are Getting in the Way of Your Business," "Your mindset can be the biggest obstacle to overcome in your business. Many people carry around a false assumption about themselves that needs to be removed or improved. In business, you are the gateway to your company."[28]

ENTREPRENEURIAL TIP

As you make the shift towards an empowered state of being, fears and doubts may arise. It is beneficial to place positive affirmation statements around you, on your desk, phone, car visor, or other places where you frequent. Also, surround yourself with supportive cheerleaders (mentors, a colleague, or a friend) who can provide you with a boost of confidence. Meet these individuals for a cup of coffee or tea. You can also practice your sales pitches in the mirror. I have done this many times with keynote speeches I am preparing, and can attest to its value.

THE BEST CHAMPION IS YOU!

"You have to be able to get up and dust yourself off and always be going forward." —Rita Moreno

A booking agent for a national television appearance with the association to NAPW (National Association of Professional Women) contacted me. She asked for a referral of a television guest who has a bestselling book and can speak on national television about their business or entrepreneurial lessons.

My response to the booking agent was, "I will speak on the topic of *Five Secrets to Build a Buzz Around Your Business or Organization.* Tell me when to be in New York City. I will get myself there. I can inspire the audience as a result of real-life experiences. But the focus will be on things I wish I did in hindsight." [29]

Tenacity confirmed the booking!

At the show's filming, I learned that other guests include best-selling Amazon authors and national speakers. I am the only woman that did not have a book to sell.

At that moment, anxiety and fear might have crippled me if I had compared my talents to those more experienced than me. Instead, I showcased self-belief. I recognized that my experiences and lessons learned could offer insight to other entrepreneurs. Overall, the television appearance was a great experience.

SELF-RELIANCE IS A TOOL FOR SUCCESS

Advancing Women, an online job board for women and diversity candidates, published an article that included these words regarding self-reliance, "Successful entrepreneurs try to take full responsibility for their actions. They know that what they are today, and what they are going to be tomorrow, and depend solely on themselves, as it is the outcome of their own choices and decisions. They are proactive people who set goals, walk an extra mile to achieve them and rely, primarily, on their resources and abilities." [30]

POINTS TO PONDER AND COMPLETE

I AM CAPABLE OF...

A LIMITED BELIEF OF MINE IS...

I CAN SHIFT THAT BELIEF BY...

Pause Point for You

"Pausing allows you to take a beat to take a breath in your life. As everybody else is rushing around like a lunatic out there, I dare you to do the opposite."
— Maria Shriver

As an entrepreneur, you manage various aspects of your business. A good practice is to ensure that you feel inner balance. Make time for you. After attaining balance, you can approach situations with clarity and strong decision-making skills.

As with any new task you aspire to do regularly, creating reminders is helpful since you may revert into old patterns of behavior. Accordingly, re-read, make sticky notes, tear out pages of books or magazines or text yourself verses or concepts you have already read that speak to you. Test drive the ideas you have learned so far.

Be mindful as you make shifts in behavior to create an ideal life; resistance will occur. So, you may need to try your choices a few times to master the feeling or action. Remember the universe is continually supporting you. Don't be critical of yourself and know that the universe has your back!

Therapist and mindfulness trainer, Rebecca Kronman emphasizes the benefits of taking time to breathe. "With just one deep breath, our attention is immediately redirected to the present moment. By taking just a few seconds to focus on the breath, we are forced to create a pause between the stimulus whatever is stressing us out at that moment and our reaction. During that pause, we notice what is happening with our thoughts and our bodies." [31]

In "Why Entrepreneurs Should Practice the Pause," Amanda Khoza tells "Multiple instances to be still with barely a thought are presented when we stop walking to let others pass, stop talking to listen, stop working to sleep, when we turn back and grab a jacket because the weather has shifted or stop because we've reached our destination. Think carefully about how you can deliberately practice your pause moments – simple ways that help you find and mind yourself better." [32]

PUT INTO ACTION - Set a reminder on your cellular phone called "Pause Time." When the reminder goes off, take five minutes to sit and breathe. Breathing is the cheapest quickest way to get connected with ourselves.

CHAPTER SEVEN

Power Thoughts Propel Energy

"Everything is energy, and that's all there is to it. Match the frequency of the reality you want, and you cannot help but get that reality. It can be no other way. This is physics."— Albert Einstein

In "How Many Thoughts Does Your Mind Think in One Hour" experts estimate that the mind thinks between 60,000 to 80,000 thoughts a day. [33] Research also shows that people spend forty-seven percent of their waking hours thinking about something other than what they're doing.[34] In other words, many of us operate on autopilot.

Do you pay attention to what you think? There is a saying: "Garbage in, Garbage out." This concept means if you think negative thoughts, you will attract the energy of that frequency.

Sometimes, our nature is to project worst-case scenarios instead of best-case outcomes. If you shift attention to an attitude of gratitude or positive thinking, energy expands to support that way of thinking for you.

CASE EXAMPLE OF ENTREPRENEURS SHARON, BETSY, AND JERRY

Let's look at what happens to Sharon who runs a business, and how thoughts influence behavior. Then, meet mindfulness teacher Betsy. Finally, visit with Jerry, who is a train wreck running his business until he shifts towards an operating practice that provides balance.

Sharon has blonde hair. She is five feet six inches tall with heels on and likes to wear black dress slacks. Sharon is a working mom and entrepreneur. Because she runs her own business, Sharon works a lot but manages to remind herself that she started the company because she desired more flexibility than her previous corporate job provided.

Jack, her husband, is a teacher. He is a support structure to Sharon and their son, Charlie. At times, Sharon forgets to be present with both of them; instead, her mind dashes to the next item on the chore list. Like many of us do when we rush to get things done and forget to be present with ourselves and others.

Sharon drives a silver Honda SUV. She listens to National Public Radio when she drives. Today, on the way home from work, she thinks to herself, "I hope Jack remembers to stop at the grocery store." Tonight, Charlie has baseball practice. As a potential vendor to Sue, a product buyer, Sharon has scheduled a conference call tonight and must stay focused. Any purchase order could mean a large buy of the company's products. Then, Sharon's family can use the profits to go on the dream vacation that they have been talking about for the past five years, a Caribbean cruise.

Sharon is usually level headed. Nevertheless, her interior dialogue shifts to negative self-talk when she is stressed. She starts to doubt her ability to sell the product and complete tasks at hand.

Have you ever paid attention to what you think when you are stressed? Or what thoughts recycle in your mind? Let's continue to see how this situation plays out for Sharon.

Jack offers verbal reassurance as soon as Sharon walks through the door, and heads to her home office. "Don't you have a conversation tonight with the purchasing agent? Just focus on why you started the company and the potential benefit for the buyer."

Immediately, Sharon adjusts her internal discussion to "I am going to nail this presentation. I create my experiences. Our company has a product that I believe in, and I can sell this product."

FOR YOU TO PONDER

WHAT IS THE DISCUSSION TAKING PLACE IN YOUR MIND? IS THE CONVERSATION UPBEAT OR SELF SABOTAGING? ARE YOU AWARE OF YOUR INTERNAL DIALOGUE?

BENEFITS OF POSITIVE THINKING

Barbara Fredrickson, a psychology professor who has written extensively about positivity, found that those who think positive thoughts have a higher capacity to take on brand new information. This then improves a person's perspective and the ability to "connect the dots," enabling them to tackle any problems and obstacles that may arise.[35]

In our case example, Sharon secures an order of 10,000 billboards as a result of the discussion with the purchasing agent. Now, fulfillment of the orders must transpire.

The following day, Sharon arrives at work and starts to think about capital investment, production timelines, staffing, etc., all the various needs of processing the new order. Then she second guesses herself and thoughts play in her head like a recording that won't stop, "You aren't capable of delivering what you promised!"

Instantly, Sharon realizes the thought is a past belief and adjusts her internal dialogue.

While you may not realize it, everyone has self-sabotaging thoughts in certain instances. Usually, these thoughts showcase themselves when you are stressed. Like a compass, your feelings help indicate when you are on track about where you want to be, your goals, or vision.[36] That is an excellent time to take a breath and recalibrate yourself.

Sharon leaves the office for a latte at *Starbucks*. While in line, she notices a flyer on the bulletin board that states, "Are you ready to silence the negative chatter and claim your potential? Join a bunch of working moms and what it means to stop doing things you hate and start doing things you love!"

Sharon grabs the flyer and rushes back to work. Later, she joins the class. Here Sharon meets Betsy who has brown hair pulled back into a ponytail and blue eyes. Betsy is the teacher of a working mom's group. Betsy welcomes everyone, "Namaste everybody. Grab a yoga mat and sit on the floor and breathe."

In the background, subtle ocean music plays. Most of the working moms can't sit more that than two minutes, including Sharon. Sharon is surprised at how difficult it is to sit quietly. Her mind starts to race once again about her to-do lists.

Jerry arrives at the class. He wears khaki pants, a blue sports coat, and a buttoned-down shirt. Jerry is good looking with olive skin and is about five foot ten inches tall. He has wavy hair. His eyes are a vibrant blue, with a green color, like a lake.

Jerry addresses the group "Hi, I'm Jerry. Betsy is my girlfriend. She wants me to speak about experiences when I have connected with myself. Betsy had me try an experiment which includes silencing the mind, listening to thoughts, and then being present with thoughts."

Jerry continues, "I never knew how busy the mind could be. Tons of thoughts race around in my mind including soccer practice, since I'm a coach, payroll at my company, projects to complete, and pretty much everything in between. Then the day rolls into another day, and I have mostly the same thoughts again."

He sips a glass of water. In a very positive tone Jerry states, "When I stop running around from place to place, I realize I need to be calmer. Especially because, as a dad, my kids count on me. Also, I run a business in the community that hopefully has a positive impact."

Jerry tells the group, "I didn't realize how busy my mind gets, especially when I feel stressed. I want to be more in balance and have clarity of mind to make the best decisions for my family and the business."

Today, a calmer, more tuned-in Jerry exists.

Jerry is the face of several entrepreneurs. He is smart and family-centric. He wants to make a difference in his community. Ideally, he longs to be the best version of himself yet has no clue how to wrestle his taskmaster persona to achieve a life in balance.

Jerry quickly learns that he can't operate at full speed all the time. He becomes aware of his behaviors and thoughts. Jerry makes a conscious choice to get back in balance. Now, he takes time in the morning to be present with himself. During the day, Jerry does a re-boot, whether he is in his car, on the road to see customers, or in his office. During this period, he takes fifteen minutes to himself and turns off all electronics. He drinks water, sits silently and breathes. He also eats healthier and loses twenty unwanted pounds by exercising three times a week. As well, Jerry practices mindfulness.

Employees begin to tell Jerry, "We can't believe how approachable you are. You are calmer and much more receptive to our ideas." Jerry's work environment flourishes. Employees feel valued. Jerry is operating from a place of balance.

In "Five Ways to Rewire Your Brain to Be Positive," author Deep Patel advises, "Start consciously taking a different approach to your thinking. One simple tip is to spend a moment calming your mind when you are feeling frazzled, stressed or distracted."[37]

HOMEWORK ASSIGNMENT – BRING AWARENESS TO WHAT YOU THINK

"Your words and thoughts have physical power."
— Will Smith

To become more conscious of your thoughts, I am asking you to explore what you think. A three-pronged approach is suggested as follows: first, develop awareness and become aware of your thought. Second is to observe your thought without judgment. Third, shift your mindset to adjust your thinking, if warranted.

Here are suggestions that serve as a vehicle to bring awareness to your thoughts and help shift consciousness towards positive thoughts.

1. Keep a log of your thoughts. For the next twenty-four hours, periodically write down your thoughts. After twenty-four hours, while you are having coffee or tea, review what you wrote and reflect on the self-observation. Be honest. Would you say any of your thoughts need fine-tuning? Are you predominately thinking positive thoughts, or limiting yourself with other ideas?

2. Use a stimulus to redirect your thoughts. An entrepreneurial friend offered a good idea: "Anytime I sense a negative thought; I pinch my earlobe. This action helps me bring awareness to what I am thinking. Then I can redirect my thoughts."

3. Founder, life coach and best-selling author Sheila Applegate teaches entrepreneurs to illuminate the

awesomeness that lies dormant within them. So, you can discover the superhuman aspects of yourself, then practically apply them to create the strongest version of yourself. Sheila offers a great modification tool in the program, Consciously Awesome.™ Folks are encouraged to wear a Consciously Awesome™ band around their wrist, and when a thought arrives that requires a shift in thinking, the person moves the band to the other wrist. This approach inspires you to be present with the thought, acknowledge the feeling of what you are thinking and then shift your consciousness.

Tip: You may want to read the article, "15 Ways Reframing Your Thoughts Can Change Your Life" found at www.rd.com/advice/relationships/reframing-your-thoughts/7/

CHAPTER EIGHT

Visualization as a Ripple Effect

"Be bold. If you are going to make an error,
make it a doozy and don't be afraid to hit
the ball." —Billy Jean King

The North American Journal of Psychology published a study reporting that athletes who practiced mental exercises or visualizations, accomplished gains in physical strength comparable to those who did the activities on weight machines. Imagine how visualization can improve performance when combined with the physical practice of seeing and believing.

MOVING TOWARDS A FRAMEWORK OF VISUALIZATION

How many of you have experienced a coach or teacher who positively influenced you? Coach Bill was my friend's father. He was about five feet ten inches tall, had brown eyes and wore glasses. Coach Bill liked to wear a baseball cap, and usually, the hat had the *Buffalo Bills* logo on it. He was even-tempered and often had a smile on his face.

Coach Bill exemplified positivity. Although years have passed, I still recall his actions and commentary. In practice exercises, "Coach" as we called him, praised us. He encouraged us to be the best version of ourselves. Coach treated everyone on equal footing and never pinned one of us against the other. He never belittled anyone. Instead, he encouraged teammates to work together to support each other.

Coach stressed the skill of using the mind to achieve a goal. He would say, "See yourself reaching the goal. Feel the goal in your bones. Visualize the achievement of the objective." Several studies show that the brain doesn't differentiate between real memory and an imagined one.

Maximum performance strategist Matt Mayberry communicates in "The Extraordinary Power of Visualizing Success," "All top performers, regardless of profession, know the importance of picturing themselves succeeding in their minds before they do so in reality. Something I have been able to translate over to the business arena from athletics is the power of visualization. It is extremely effective when harnessed and used correctly." [38]

At a very young age, I acquired a valuable business and life lesson; the desired outcome is a thought away. Feeling the desired outcome can help attract the energy as a reality.

Christopher Taibbi reveals in "How Visualization Affects the Mind" that the subconscious mind can perceive an event as real. "To our subconscious mind, imagination is real. By that I mean it can't differentiate an imagined event from a real event and considers both as the same. Therefore, whatever it is that you visualize or imagine, your subconscious thinks it is happening."[39]

"As an entrepreneur, you can utilize the concept of picturing an outcome before it becomes a reality. Visualization is a "technique involving focusing on positive mental images to achieve a particular goal." This technique can apply to virtually any goal that involves human performance." [40]

SEE IT. BELIEVE IT. FEEL IT. – A MINDSET

"Everything you can imagine is real."
—Pablo Picasso

While at the local coffee shop, I saw a flyer about a women's leadership conference. As soon as I picked up the brochure, I instinctively felt the longing to speak at the conference. I believed that the universe would perfectly align this opportunity for me.

When I arrived home, I immediately taped up the conference flyer on the refrigerator. I placed a picture of myself on the flyer and wrote, "Laura Ponticello inspires audiences with her talk 'Five Secrets to Build a Buzz around Your Business.'" Then, I started to develop a PowerPoint presentation with an outline of remarks for the speech.

To reiterate, I had not received a request to speak; still, I knew that the universe would arrange for me to speak at the conference. I began to imagine myself speaking from a podium at the conference. I said the speech out loud daily as if I was there talking to the audience. Within thirty days, I intersected with a woman who was the event organizer for the conference. As a result, I ended up speaking at the seminar, "Women Successfully Connecting in Business." This experience affirmed for me, the influence of the mind has on creating realities.

Sara Blakely, the Founder of *Spanx*, is a fan of visualization. As she puts it, "I believe you can take mental snapshots of your future, and what success looks like to you," she has said. "If you mentally see yourself in a scenario, you'll start to make decisions in your life that get you there."[41]

PUT INTO PRACTICE

Picture yourself achieving a goal and be as detailed as possible in your visual. Maybe it's giving a speech, landing a big client, or getting your product into a primary chain warehouse. The most important aspect of visualization is to feel the feeling as if the vision is happening in the present moment.

CHAPTER NINE

Jump Start the Day with Affirmations

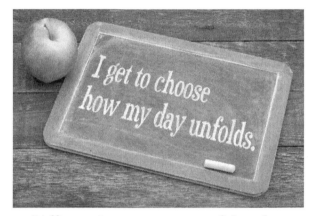

"Affirmations are a powerful tool to install desired beliefs about yourself deliberately." —Nikki Carnevale

You will interact with all different walks of life. Therefore, wouldn't it be great if you set the tone for your day on a positive note and planted the seeds for your dreams? Be mindful of your thoughts.

While you can't control other people's behaviors, you can decide how best to react to situations. When I start the day on a positive note; I find it is easier to deal with the day's interactions. One easy way to jump-start the day on an upbeat note is while you take a shower, use that time to repeat affirmations or intentions.

Intentions that are positive statements said in the present moment help reinforce the desired outcome in your mind. Positive affirmations allow you to replace your negativity, one thought at a time![42]

My first exposure to affirmations was early in my business career. I had also played sports in high school and college, so I firmly understood the impact of using visualization for goal attainment. This understanding permitted me to expand a belief system in support of the concept that <u>you can create your own experience.</u>

Then about fifteen years ago, I attended "I Can Do It" a conference held in San Diego, California with a dear friend who ran a non-profit organization. I listened firsthand to Louise Hay when I sat in the first row at the conference. Louise is considered a pioneer in the affirmation movement.

"The secret to having your affirmations work quickly and consistently is to prepare an atmosphere for them to grow in. Affirmations are like seeds planted in soil. Poor soil, poor growth. Rich soil, abundant growth. The more you choose to think thoughts that make you feel good, the quicker the affirmations work."
— Louise Hay, *The Power of Affirmations*[43]

Another forerunner in the personal transformation movement is New York Times bestselling author Wayne Dyer whose work greatly influenced my personal and professional success. Wayne states, "My favorite affirmation when I feel stuck or out of sorts is: Whatever I need is already here, and it is all for my highest good. Jot this down and post it conspicuously throughout your home, on the dashboard of your car, at your office, on your microwave oven, perhaps even near your toilets!

Remind yourself: I live in a friendly universe that will support anything I desire that is aligned with the universal source of all."[44]

In observing successful entrepreneurs, a constant practice seems to be the power of positivity; precisely, the ability to see past challenges and move towards solutions. In doing so, those who have spent time envisioning the future, and practicing daily intentions surrounding key goals and actions – seem to yield higher results. The bottom line is where we place our attention draw forth the energy to support desires.

FOR YOU TO PUT INTO PRACTICE

Take five minutes at the start and end of every day to write down and say out loud positive intentions. Ideally, try to be consistent. You may find value in the video, How To Attract What You Want which can be accessed at www.youtube.com/watch?v=XicKygU-g1s

Morning Business Chat podcast offers a good affirmation, "I believe in myself and trust in my abilities to succeed in all I do."[45]

THE BENEFITS OF BEING OPTIMISTIC

"I believe the last thing I read at night will likely manifest when I'm sleeping. You become what you think about the most." —Daymond John

Optimistic people tend to be healthier, more productive, and generally happier than those who view themselves less positively. One study shows that after four weeks of repeated self-affirmations, participants experienced an increase in their mental well-being. [46]

CHAPTER TEN

Pause Long Enough to Notice

"One of the most tragic things I know about human nature is that all of us tend to put off living. We are all dreaming of some magical rose garden over the horizon instead of enjoying the roses that are blooming outside our windows today."— Dale Carnegie

My mother in law, Flo has said to me: "Take time to stop and smell the roses!" She wanted to emphasize that despite how busy the day's occurrences might be, it's important to take time to slow down and enjoy life.

Is the following scenario familiar to you? You are in line at *McDonald's, Panera,* or another place with a drive-thru window. You place a drink or food order. You hope there isn't a long line. While in line, you begin to think about a subsequent errand, or you check text messages. You receive the takeout order quickly and drive away.

Next, you rush back to work or move on to another item on your to-do list. In the midst of everything, you neglected to notice the tree that was flowering next to the drive-thru window. You forgot to use those three moments spent while waiting in the drive-thru line to take a deep breath and still your mind. You missed out on noticing things or experiences in your peripheral view. For example, you didn't see the girl with the infectious smile waiving as you peel out of the drive-thru line. Also, you bypass the fact that free car washes are available in the parking lot as a thank you to customers.

If you are a parent, your child or children might have been in the drive-thru line with you. How great would it have been to share a few moments when everyone is off their electronic devices, and you converse! Also, you could teach your children and perhaps their friends why stillness if a good thing, that to be present with yourself is a healthy choice.

If you were driving by yourself or en route home from work, you could have pulled the car over for three to five minutes to "stop and smell the roses" by being present with yourself. Similarly, if you commute to work, the train or subway might provide ample time for you to sit listening to inspirational music through head-phones while you take a few minutes to unwind.

HOW MINDFULNESS IS MAKING ENTREPRENEURS BETTER LEADERS

The article "How Mindfulness is Making Entrepreneurs Better Leaders" tells us, "Business owners can benefit from allocating just two to five minutes in the morning to sitting down and practicing this." Additionally, "Taking time out to exhale can give you a greater sense of clarity and focus and help you avoid explosive situations and manage your working day in a stress-free way."[47]

WHY SELF CARE IS IMPORTANT

"Why Self Care Needs to Be Your Number 1 Strategy" includes the following information: "It's not unusual to strike out at work when you're barely holding it together. It's hard enough to get up to bat when you're in a haze, let alone hit a home run. It's more likely that you'll hit a home run when you can see clearly, feel strong and have your wits about you."[48]

For the men's health article "Perceptions from Around the Globe" 16,000 men were surveyed, and it was found that the role that self-care can play in enabling men to take greater control and improving their health should be further explored. Self-care could allow men to treat diseases, injuries, and health conditions while giving them the opportunity to prevent future health problems, reduce ailments and increase the quality of life.[49]

WHEN YOU GO OFF KILTER - HOW TO REBALANCE

"What good is meeting our goal if we are dry, and tired and empty when we get there?"
— Piglet character from *Winnie the Pooh*

Bob ran from one client meeting to another meeting. 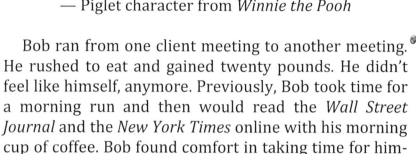 He rushed to eat and gained twenty pounds. He didn't feel like himself, anymore. Previously, Bob took time for a morning run and then would read the *Wall Street Journal* and the *New York Times* online with his morning cup of coffee. Bob found comfort in taking time for himself at the onset of the day.

As time passed, work demands piled high. Bob stopped running and neglected any self-care time. Now, work consumed most of Bob's time. Bob is like many entrepreneurs who desperately desire time for themselves but due to work demands, forgo balancing life practices.

I intersected with Bob at the local bakery. He was tall with salt and pepper hair color, and he wore a pinned stripped shirt with a solid colored tie. Bob's body language displayed that he was in a hurry. He tapped his foot at a rapid, forceful pace. While in line, he told me his story.

Rolling his eyes, Bob introduced himself as the Vice President of a financial service firm. He presented his business card and revealed that his clients are demanding!

I inquired, "Bob, what do you do to care for yourself?"

"You mean like read the newspaper to see what's going on in the world while I gulp coffee and check my emails for the day? I used to go running!" said Bob.

I laughed and responded, "Could you read the newspaper while sipping coffee instead of being in a race to finish it?" "Why did you stop running?"

Then I asked, "Did you have knee problems?"

"No, I can't make that kind of time anymore. I don't have that kind of time." Bob enquired how much longer the wait for service at the bakery would be.

I advised, "When you slow down at the onset of the day – you permit yourself to be present. If you rush, you set the pace for the day. The more you are in balance, the more you have a feeling of calmness to face what the day brings. You will have more energy for clients if you are mindful of having life in balance practices. Overall you will feel happier."

Bob responded, "While I appreciate your commentary. Most likely I will keep doing what I have been doing." Nonetheless, he then inquired, "How do I get a copy of your book?".

I am not attached to whether Bob read the book. There is a common theme in this incident that relates to current entrepreneurs. Many entrepreneurs feel precisely like Bob and think, "I've lost perspective. Life has become work and more work."

Bob most likely has taken one of two directions. He continued to live "as is, status quo" with stress building up over time or some occurrence pushed Bob to amend his immediate behavior; hopefully, it was sooner than later.

TELLTALE SIGNS OF BEING OUT OF BALANCE

- You are revved up. You can't quiet the mind.
- You run from place to place without entirely being present or accomplishing what you set out to do.
- You lose sight of what matters. You forgo any self-care time and are inconsistent with healthy practices. You run to the point of exhaustion.
- You are short tempered with others, exhibit angst and become frustrated quickly.
- You lack clarity needed for decision-making abilities, and judgment is clouded.

"When you experience stress, it is easy to fall out of balance, yet that is precisely when you need to recharge and reboot." — Shelly, a thriving mother, and entrepreneur.

QUICK TIP TO RECHARGE
PUT INTO PRACTICE

Seek refuge in nature. Go outside for ten minutes. Breathe in the air. Take a walk or sit down, outside if possible. Among office workers, even the view of nature through a window is associated with lower stress and higher job satisfaction. [50]

"The relationship with yourself sets the tone for every other relationship you have." — Jane Travis

CHAPTER ELEVEN

Pay Attention to the Tea Leaves

"Tea time is a chance to slow down, pull
back and appreciate our surroundings."
—Letitia Baldridge

Dr. Jill Little was a professor. As a teacher, Jill witnessed students and colleagues who ran from place to
place instead of observing their surroundings. Jill
shared, "If you don't slow the pace, you will never connect with you. You'll forget to be quiet. When you are
still, you can hear inner wisdom and feel intuition."

Jill's home library was rich with painted cabinets. She
was an avid reader and collected books from around the
world. Jill had over five hundred books from various

philosophers, spiritual authors, and teachers. Jill was also an author of six books.

Jill told me, "The universe is constantly sending you signals. The problem is you are too busy to notice what is near you or in front of you."

One of my favorite experiences with Jill was sharing a cup of tea while we talked. Every conversation began with Jill praying over the drink. She infused an intention into the tea, "Today we ask the tea to infuse us with wisdom, knowledge and to help us to be present with the tea."

I believed the tea leaves offered us guidance, and so did Jill. She recited a passage from a book that she was inspired to pull from her library. We intermittently discussed the meaning and relevance of life, while she read.

Every time, I left Jill's presence, I felt like the "sunshine was present" inside of the tea leaves that we shared.

What does this have to do you? Jill's husband was a self-made millionaire. In many instances, like many of us, her husband fixated on things to be completed instead of being present in the current conversation, to enjoy the current moment.

When was the last time you were fully present in a conversation? Would a customer, staff member, or family member concur about you being present - not just being physically present but as a participant in the discussion at hand, without distractions?

PUT IN PRACTICE

HOW CAN YOU MAKE THE ACT OF BEING PRESENT IN A CONVERSATION, A MORE FREQUENT OCCURRENCE?

Time passed, and Jill abruptly died of a brain aneurysm.

Today, I feel Jill's presence when I slow down to be present with a cup of tea. I close my eyes and envision us sharing a cup of tea from a golden chalice. We search for wisdom in the tea leaves. When I open my eyes, I acknowledge that Jill's knowledge is forever with me, even though her physical presence is in Heaven.

You can learn more about Jill's writings in the books, *Sharing the Medicine of Love* and *Ihood: a GPS for Living* which are available on Amazon.com

BENEFIT OF BEING PRESENT

"The secret of health for both mind and body is not to mourn for the past, nor to worry about the future, but to live the present moment wisely and earnestly." — Buddha

Executive coach Gayle Ely in "Three Ways Being Present in the Moment can Benefit Your Business" highlights, "Being present at the moment allows us to harness all our energy to focus on what is in front of us right now. Focused energy allows for more laser-like precision aimed at the task at hand, which results in better outcomes."[51]

"I recharge myself every day at 3:00 pm. I find that as the day progresses, due the constant customer calls and staff interaction, I need to pause for a few minutes and recharge. I go into my office, close the door and drink a big glass of water. Then I take a few breathes, stand up and stretch. This recharge pause helps me greatly." — Jim, entrepreneur.

CHAPTER TWELVE

Follow Your Passions

"Follow your bliss and the universe will
open doors where there were only walls."
—Joseph Campbell

What makes you happy? Are you passionate about the work you perform?

Bestselling author Shannon Kaiser in the article "3 Unexpected Ways to Find Your Passionate Purpose," offers insight, "Ask yourself what you love. Start taking steps to do what you love. When you are inspired and connected to your happy self, inspiration floods your heart and soul. When you lead from your heart, you are naturally more joyful and motivated to explore. By doing what you love, you will be inspired and gain insights into what brings you the most joy."[52]

"NO MATTER HOW MUCH MONEY YOU MAKE, NOTHING WILL HELP YOU OVERCOME THE FEELING OF DOING SOMETHING YOU HATE."[53]

Business.com states, "You will manage to achieve business success only if you have a passion for the work that you are doing and can create real value for your customers. Through your passion, you will either support your business or break it. It is easy to recognize people with real passion for what they are doing. We prefer to work with such individuals or companies because we trust their passion will be something which will result in our business success."

FIND ENJOYMENT IN THE WORK YOU PERFORM

"Don't get caught up in chasing the dollar, find enjoyment in what you do. Something that makes you jump out of bed every morning – and do it all again."
— Mike, an experienced entrepreneur.

Mike operates a successful contracting and heating and air conditioning business for thirty years. He conveys "I love my customers. Each day I wake up with excitement to see what the day brings. I have a passion for my customers and business."

"I enjoy the fact that I have an intimate relationship with customers. I enjoy getting to know their families and hearing about their challenges and successes. The customers take an interest in knowing me and asking about my family, and business. As a result, there isn't anything I wouldn't do for a customer. That is why I go the extra mile for customers. They don't expect it, but I do. Because of this passion for customers, they refer business."

Mike advises: "As a small business entrepreneur, grow the customer base you want, then build and maintain a solid relationship with them. Success and wealth will follow. This is a long-term investment."

I ask Mike, *"What inspired you to start the business?"*

He responds, "I worked very hard for a company when I started in this business. I got very good at doing what I did and fine-tuning my craft."

I thought, "If I am going to put that kind of passion into working for another person, I might as well start a business. It was the best decision that I could have made for my family and me."

Mike's passion goes beyond his work. He loves to ride dirt bikes and over the years has advanced his skills in this area. His love of motorsports takes him across the country to different venues, and he created a motocross course as well.

DON'T WASTE TIME ON A JOB YOU HATE

Mikes advice continues, "Live life and don't waste days doing a job you hate. Don't forget about your health along the way - stay fit mentally and physically. Exercise will help keep stress levels under control."

IS PASSION GOOD FOR BUSINESS?

Mike Kapel contributing writer to the article "Is Passion Good for Business" reveals, "Passion is what drives you. Passion keeps you going despite the difficulties that your business will inevitably come across. I had many opportunities to throw up my arms and simply give up, but my passion caused me to keep going. I couldn't think about anything but making my business succeed."[54]

TEST THE WATERS

You may be a passionate entrepreneur who thrives while running your business. Or you may not love your work. If you are not passionate about your job, there may be economics that keeps you there. However, you can explore other options. If you are pondering starting another business – spend time in a discovery phase, during which you equip yourself with knowledge. Talk to experts in the area, investigate the competition, and explore what it would take to obtain capital investments.

If you have a full-time job and are dabbling in a part-time business as an entrepreneur, maybe it's time for you to step forward and commit fully to your entrepreneurial desires. I am not advocating that you quit your day job, though, it may be necessary at some point to focus your energy on what provides you the most joy.

If you are coasting along and desire expansion outside of your work, seek out what makes you happy. Hobbies can be passions as our seasoned entrepreneur has shared. His hobby of motor cross racing became his passion.

As mentioned earlier in the book, it is our human nature to desire expansion. Growing is part of the human experience. Therefore, explore possibilities. Local community colleges have program offerings that you can investigate. Meet with an industry expert in the field you want to discover. Seek insight from those who have experience in your area of interest. If you are knowledgable in your work field, it is terrific to mentor newbies in your area of expertise.

Research indicates that middle-aged individuals are more likely to make successful transitions experientially rather than analytically. Big revelations come from jumping in and trying new things to see what works.[55]

TEACH CHILDREN TO EXPLORE PASSIONS

"You can't be that kid standing at the top of the waterslide, overthinking it. You have to go down the chute." —Tina Fey

As a young girl, I loved to read and write. If you looked around my bedroom at that time, you would notice books stacked everywhere. One favorite book, *Little Women*, was on the nightstand. A beloved character in book *Little Women* is named Jo. Jo has intellect and tenacity. She is fearless and feels that life is an adventure to discover and explore. She ventures off to start her writing career during a period which odds didn't favor woman writers. I secretly wanted to be like Jo.

Think about a favorite pastime or passion from childhood. What were you drawn towards and what brought you the most happiness?

Life is interesting. As we age, we can lose the gift of childlike wonderment. Also, we forget about the things we loved in our childhood that we may still want to explore. In our adult ways of thinking, attachment to specific outcomes takes place instead of having fun and enjoying the current times, as kids do. As a result, we may relinquish doing things we love, which can be any number of things, such as, gardening, running, hockey, painting, flying, or roller skating.

"Why We Should Teach Our Kids Entrepreneurship at a Young Age" highlights "Cultivating entrepreneurship in the young is vital, as children are born imaginative, energetic, and willing to take risks, but without entrepreneurial education, the enterprising spirit of children dramatically declines over time and is almost nonexistent by the time they graduate from high school."[56]

PUT INTO PRACTICE

Consider encouraging your child, niece, nephew, or perhaps a co-worker's teenage son or daughter to explore areas of interest. Offer to let young adults shadow you for a day. Encourage them to enroll in creative programs offered after school or during the summer to examine entrepreneurialism.

CHAPTER THIRTEEN

A Warehouse of Creative Energy

"Whatever you focus on expands."
—Pam Grout

What if an unlimited resource of knowledge existed to help you? And all that you would need to do is open the floodgate to creative energy for idea generation? Within you resides a warehouse of creativity. Creative energy is ever-flowing, expansive and limitless. As the gate to your creativity opens, idea formations, product inventions and collaborative efforts surrounding original endeavors emerge.

New York Times bestselling author, physician, and teacher, Deepak Chopra says "What I'm suggesting is that everyone needs a supply of energy that is renewable, vibrant, unstressful and uplifting. Such an energy supply is within you."[57]

TAPPING INTO CREATIVE ENERGY

Have you ever witnessed how syrup is extracted from a maple tree? You must "tap into" the maple tree to draw out the sugar. The syrup does not magically jump out of the tree into the bucket to collect the syrup. Creative energy works the same! The more you extract, the more the bucket that collects the syrup is filled. A fundamental requirement is you must tap into the energy. You are capable of igniting your creativity by bringing awareness to and exploring this aspect of yourself.

Let's look to an additional example to make a point. To illuminate a light, you must turn on the light! Inventiveness intensifies as you access creative energy. A vital requirement is that *you must tune and tap into the essence of the inner compass.*

YOU MIGHT WANT TO EXPLORE READING MORE ON THIS SUBJECT AT:
http://www.oprah.com/oprahs-lifeclass/your-energy-is-infinite-and-this-is-why/all#ixzz58cjrZsv3

B2B staff writer, Sammi Carmela, emphasizes in "Why Creativity Matters Most to Entrepreneurs" that "Everyone has creative potential, and the creative thought process can be improved and strengthened. Learning new hobbies and skills is an excellent way to lay down new neural networks but learning a new art form is one of the best methods to train the mind in developing creative problem-solving skills. The arts require the use of divergent thinking." [58]

WHY CREATIVITY IS IMPORTANT

CLEVERISM Magazine featured in the online article "Why Creativity is so Crucial for Entrepreneurs" that "Creativity helps us think of ways to improve existing business practices. A brand might be very established and popular among consumers, but there is always something that can be done differently and in a better way. A creative mind is like an artist who invents new and exciting patterns on canvas. Creativity is what ignites unthinkable ideas and bring innovation into existing practices." [59]

PUT INTO PRACTICE

Surrounding yourself with other creative thinkers is a great way to get your brain in the fast lane. By surrounding yourself with other creative people, whether they excel in writing, music, or art forms, can help propel your creativity.[60]

HOW CREATIVITY INFUSES INTO WORK ENVIRONMENTS

When I worked in Silicon Valley, the office environment was super conducive to creativity. The engineers were creators and visionaries. They excelled at seeing beyond the current state of technology to "imagine" new product enhancements, inventions or ways of doing business. One of the inspiring things I witnessed during the creative process was a free for all of idea sharing. The work environment encouraged staff members to explore diverse ideas, and not to be attached to one approach over another, thereby, allowing ideas to flow freely.

The workers knew how to tap into creative energy. They were fearless in attempting various ways to ignite creativity and idea generation. As a result, one person served as a domino effect for another person to generate ideas.

NOTES FROM MY TIME IN SILICON VALLEY

A whiteboard evolved where people listed ideas minus any judgments or limitations surrounding beliefs. Colorful magic markers transferred people's thoughts onto the whiteboard as employees scribed ideas. The colors of the office walls were vibrant, not plastered with white paint as is the case of many sterile work environments. Bright, bold shades of yellow, blue and purple, engulfed the workspaces. Plants were everywhere. Living things added energy to the work atmosphere.

The engineering, marketing and sales team members placed sticky notes, concepts, and diagrams on the whiteboard in the community brainstorming space. Collectively ideas streamed together like a kite flying in the wind. Dialogue occurred around how the concepts could develop into realities.

No one belittled any idea. Instead, creativity existed in the purest form. There were no limits to any ideas.

People wore t-shirts with Bob Marley's image printed on them or other favorite bands.

I looked ridiculous in a blue suit.

Tacos and pizza were allowed in the workspace. Team members worked through the night, and into the dawn hours or when inspiration transpired. The company had a kitty jar where everyone placed their spare change, and the money was used once a month to pay for group pizza and tacos.

Creativity thrives beyond the average nine-to-five workday. When ideas flow, they flow. The outcome of creativity is incredible because work is supposed to be fun. The staff I worked with played foosball and threw darts. They laughed, made fun of each other and celebrated their work progress.

Everyone served as idea generators for one another, like light plugs being placed into electric outlets. What a positive environment!

FOR REFLECTION

WHAT IS ONE THING YOU CAN DO TO JUMP-START YOUR CREATIVITY?

A FEW SUGGESTIONS TO KICK START IMAGINATION AND CREATIVITY FROM THE YOUNG ENGINEERS THAT I OBSERVED IN SILICON VALLEY

- Go to the movies and seek out animated films. Have a play day with a best friend, co-worker or yourself. "Take a day or even a few hours off and go somewhere that inspires you."[61]
- Colors enhance creativity. Paint or place color in the workplace. Actor Jim Carey speaks about his path using color as a fuel for the imagination in an inspiring video available. https://vimeo.com/226379658
- Stretch. Move. Get the blood flowing.

Phoebe Cade Miles, board president and CEO of the Cade Museum and daughter of Gatorade inventor Dr. James Robert Cade, is a believer in the power of creativity. She watched her father work tirelessly to invent a product that, five decades after its introduction, is still used by athletes around the world.

"The invention of Gatorade is a perfect example of a creative collision," Cade Miles told *Business News Daily*. "It took experts from two seemingly unrelated subjects, nephrology, and football, to bring about a completely new category of sports beverages." [62]

CREATIVE LIFE LESSONS

"Think left and think right and think low and think high.
Oh, the things you can think up if you only try."
—Dr. Seuss

Entrepreneurs forget to be kids at heart. When you play creatively, you experience childlike wonder and creativity unfolds. You must grant yourself time to have fun! Fun can incorporate into work; these don't have to be independent concepts. Happy and inspired employees are the ones that will most likely be innovative and productive. This outcome begins with making work an enjoyable place to be.[63]

After returning from my time working in Silicon Valley, I was devoted to infusing fun and creativity into the work environment. As Monster.com, a global online job solution highlights, "If people are having fun, they're going to work harder, stay longer, maintain their composure in a crisis and take better care of the organization."
[64]

PUT INTO PRACTICE – TAKE ACTION

Consider doing a fun staff activity such as paintball, yoga, or watching for dolphins on a pier. Think outside of the box. Ask your staff for ideas. To read an article about stimulating ideas for team building, visit: www.snacknation.com/blog/teambuilding-activies-for-work

CHAPTER FOURTEEN

Intuition is our Friend

"Don't you dare underestimate the power
of your own instinct."
— Barbara Corcoran

Merriam-Webster dictionary defines intuition in three ways: First as an "immediate apprehension or cognition without reasoning or inferring," second, "knowledge or conviction gained by intuition," and third, "the power or faculty of attaining direct knowledge or perception without evident rational thought and inference."

Psychology Today reveals, "As a culture, we have learned to believe that rationality is what should prevail when making decisions about anything from crucial business mergers to what to eat for lunch. But what of that "inner voice," that gut feeling, that little something instinctual from within that tells us how we feel beneath those layers of logic?"[65]

How do you decipher the difference between what feels like a gut sensation and an internal pulling towards a decision versus the use of logic to make a rational choice?

LOGIC VERSUS INTUITION IN DECISION MAKING

Researchers at <u>Leeds</u> say that such natural feelings or intuitions are real, and we should take our hunches seriously. According to a team led by Professor Gerard Hodgkinson of the Centre for Organisational Strategy, Learning and Change at Leeds University Business School, intuition is the result of the way our brains store, process and retrieves information on a subconscious level and so is a real psychological phenomenon that needs further study to help us harness its potential. [66]

A healthy balance exists between exercising logic and utilizing intuition for decision making. Decisions made in haste, usually do not lead to the outcomes that an individual expects. Think about times when your inner voice said to take a different direction, or you had a gut feeling that an occurrence would take place before it happened.

"There are 100 million neurons, and every class of neurotransmitter in your gut is used to process external stimuli and send signals to your brain. The brain translates these signals, so we can make decisions and act. It also edits, censures, and resists some of the data it receives especially if emotions are triggered. We all have intuition, yet we don't consciously listen to it, trusting only what appears to be rational in our often irrational mind."[67]

FOR REFLECTION

Have there been times in your life when a gut feeling or sensation existed, yet you ignored it to err on the side of logic? How can you become mindful of using intuition as a gauge point for decision making?

As the article "7 Attributes of Intuitive Business Leaders" notes, "The ability to be creative, think on the fly and make key business decisions with little time amidst the tsunami of external information is vital. Intuition is the natural intelligence that allows us to see ahead of the curve, to generate innovative ideas, to communicate powerfully and to do so without having to study spreadsheets or gather piles of data."[68]

"The real challenge is not whether to trust intuition, but how to strengthen it to make it more trustworthy." — Gary Klein, Ph.D., *The Power of Intuition: How to Use Your Gut to Make Better Decisions at Work*[69]

A CASE EXAMPLE: USING INTUITION IN BUSINESS DEALINGS

Kathy worked for me indirectly. She was bright, enthusiastic and a go-getter though she needed time to develop her intuitive wisdom. She had trained in marketing at an undergraduate level. One of Kathy's strengths is that she was very good at helping companies connect with their demographic.

Let's focus on an example of where Kathy disregarded intuitive signs. In hindsight, she should have paid attention to that gut feeling resurfaced within her.

In college, due to the demands of her degree's academic requirements, she learned to use logic to solve problems. Kathy was taught to prioritize logic and didn't learn anything in school about tapping into her intuition for decision making.

Kathy was assigned to develop and implement a social marketing campaign. My client had hired Kathy to launch their new line of products. During the client meeting in which Kathy presented her marketing plan, I happened to notice that my stomach felt like it was turning an opposite direction when Kathy spoke about timelines for campaign implementation.

I politely excused myself to use the bathroom. I breathed and tuned in to see how I was feeling about the situation. Immediately, I sensed that what Kathy planned to implement wasn't going to work for this client.

Logic told Kathy the deployment plan was perfect. She had successfully installed a marketing plan for another client with similar demographics. That campaign was a huge success. A missing variable in this equation was the current client's behavior is unpredictable. The client, Suzie, was a control freak, and most likely she would expect immediate results, and this campaign needed time to work correctly.

Kathy's presentation sounded good on the surface. Nevertheless, a prevailing thought of mine was that Suzie wouldn't be patient enough to wait and see the results of the campaign, she would want immediate results.

I met Kathy for a cup of tea after the presentation meeting and shared reservations about whether Suzie would allocate the time necessary for the campaign to run its' course. I communicated to Kathy, "Tests for you lie ahead with the current plan."

Kathy politely thanked me for insight and said, "History with a similar client showed me that this social media campaign if implemented properly, will work. I am moving forward with the plan, I presented."

That evening, I didn't sleep.

The campaign began, and two weeks passed. Suzie started to text Kathy saying, "I expected more results by this point." Kathy's campaign was a 90-day cycle before any results could be measured. Overall, I identified that Kathy could not deliver results within a timeline that Suzie felt was reasonable. There was a gap in customer expectations.

I spoke with Suzie and explained that her expectations might be unrealistic, and she needed to be patient. Suzie demanded results. Kathy was unable to meet expectations. Kathy offered to refund Suzie's consultant fee. I attempted to bridge the gap, but Suzie was determined to fire Kathy and hired another firm.

Afterward, Kathy stated that when she was in the initial meeting with Suzie where she presented the plan, she had a gut feeling of conflict; still logic told her to continue based on historical data.

"I had an uncomfortable feeling, though I couldn't understand the feeling. I brushed it off as nervous energy," said Kathy.

I explained to Kathy, "While logic is excellent to obtain facts and make educated decisions, it's best always to check in to see if the situation or the client is right for you. It's helpful to take a deep breath and tune in with your body to see how you are feeling about the impending decision. Using intuition as a gauge point, you can then write down the question for which you are seeking clarity. It is only when you have an interconnection with yourself that you can glean insight on decisions."

Intuition helps you act from instinct, not impulse; it's a "look before you leap" type of wisdom that points you to positive energy.

LESSONS FOR AN ENTREPRENEUR

"I have found when signals such as gut feelings or intense reactions to certain situations occur; I need to pay attention. Within those moments, I ask myself "Is this the right decision for me and the business? — A leader who runs a consulting firm.

In "Why All Successful Business People Use Their Intuition," one tip presented to us is to "Listen to your inner hunches to always pay attention to your gut feeling about something. Even if it seems illogical to do something, your intuition is trying to tell you there is an unforeseen factor that is going to make this a disaster for you. Start following your instinct and get into the habit of checking in with yourself. Ask yourself regularly, does this feel right? Does this feel wrong?" [70]

CHAPTER FIFTEEN

Resilience and Community Engagement

"I'm convinced that about half of what separates the successful entrepreneurs from the non-successful ones is pure perseverance." — Steve Jobs

One-character trait common among entrepreneurs is resilience. You may experience opposing times when your business is in flux; perhaps grants will be hard to secure, or economic impact project commitments and staff turnover may feel overwhelming. That said, resilience is a crucial component of success.

Resilience is the capacity to recover quickly from difficulties and overcome adversity. Psychologists have identified some of the factors that make someone resilient, among them is a positive attitude, optimism, the ability to regulate emotions, and see failure as a form of helpful feedback. Even after misfortune, resilient people are blessed with the outlook that they can change course and soldier on. [71]

A pair of Spanish psychologists have written about the three dimensions of resilience — hardiness, resourcefulness, and optimism — and how these factors helped the average entrepreneur catapult a business towards the distant, successful horizon. Not only is your resilience a predictor of your success, but it's also one of the most critical factors. [72]

"Resilience is the virtue that enables people to move through hardship and become better. No one escapes pain, fear, and suffering. From pain can come wisdom, from fear can come courage. From suffering can come strength if we have the virtue of resilience."[73]

Businesses have ebbs and flows. There are days when things line up correctly and other days when you want to pull out your hair due to frustration. Entrepreneurs are a resilient bunch. When you struggle, remind yourself of what served as the impetus to start your company in the first place and consider what motivates you to work today.

POINT TO PONDER

WHAT SERVES AS MOTIVATION FOR YOU ON
THE DAYS WHEN YOU EXPERIENCE
FRUSTRATION?

AS YOU THINK ABOUT MOTIVATORS FOR FUELING YOUR DESIRES, IT IS HELPFUL TO PLACE REMINDERS AROUND YOU

"An image of my kids on my cellular phone serves as a positive motivator on days when I am frustrated. I view the screenshot a few times. Then I think of a future goal we can do as a family, and this thought propels me ahead." — Bob, a retail store owner.

As you make the shift from frustration to joy, you will find that there are tools to help you. Daily reminders can serve as catalysts for motivation. Reminders can include motivational quotes on your desk or an inspirational image placed in some space that you access often. As well encircle yourself with a real champion or people who are encouraging.

"I tend to listen to podcasts or YouTube meditations in the morning, and this practice helps set a positive tone for the day" shares Susan, a former client.

One interesting observation I've made in coaching entrepreneurs is that when they are giving back to others, they find purpose in their work.

COMMUNITY ENGAGEMENT

"Good entrepreneurs are community builders, actively involved with their communities and dedicated to the community's wellbeing. If you're dedicated to your community, it will be dedicated to you."
— Robert Kiyosaki

I am a big believer that what you give out to the universe comes back to you a thousand-fold — a Jesuit college education that me that in serving others you attain fulfillment, too. As a result of my family roots and Jesuit teachings in college, I learned the value of helping others.

As I spent time in the corporate world, I soon became aware that not everyone has a giving philosophy. There is nothing wrong with the mentality of "I want to help my family first," nevertheless you are part of a broader community.

Community engagement goes beyond the concept of a tithe which is giving a particular portion of pay to another person or a cause. In running companies, you may choose to sponsor an event or volunteer at an event. Today's generation validates that employees want to engage with causes that speak to their hearts socially.

COLLECTIVELY HELPING OTHERS

During her senior year, my niece led a coin collection drive to raise money for the Syracuse Rescue Mission, which helps homeless people, including women and children. Each college dormitory collected their leftover coins from buying coffee or beer during the year and annually turned in the coins for cash which they then donated to the organization and helped the local community.

In a study conducted by Harris Interactive with Ernest Young, sixty-two percent of respondents believe that giving back makes their companies stronger in the long run. In today's world, the younger generation of workers wants work environments who give back and are focused on community engagement.[74]

FOR REFLECTION

WHEN WAS THE LAST TIME YOU PARTICIPATED IN A COMMUNITY SERVICE ACTIVITY WITH EMPLOYEES OR CUSTOMERS?

HAVE YOU EVER VOLUNTEERED WITH FRIENDS OR FAMILY MEMBERS IN THE COMMUNITY?

Osprey Packs, an outdoor company specializing in technical packs and travel gear, has thirty-three team members. Its Volunteer Incentive Program has become an essential part of Osprey's benefits package. In 2007, each employee was given one day to spend volunteering with a charity of their choice. The program managed by the HR team offers organized volunteer opportunities, ranging from trail restorations to river clean-ups.[75]

CHAPTER SIXTEEN

Our Words and Actions

"Your words have power use them
wisely." —Anonymous

Charlie or "Dad" as I will refer to him here, is an entrepreneur at heart. He is hardworking and has only missed a handful of work days in his lifetime. Dad has worn many different hats. Besides being a strong, resilient man for his family, he was the Vice President of Sales for home decoration and jewelry company and owned a painting business. Now as a bartender, Dad counsels many patrons in various aspects of their lives. Dad knows how to deal with customers and conveys good advice.

DAD'S THREE GOLDEN RULES:

1. Words have meaning. <u>Choose words wisely.</u> The impact you can make on an employee, customer, or mother sitting on the sidelines for the Little League game (who might be a future customer) can affect an individual negatively or positively.

2. <u>No one defines your self-worth but you!</u> Dad communicates, "You alone are responsible for how you view yourself. Don't let what other people say about you determine your worth."

Entrepreneurial Tip: Develop a pattern of self-talk that validates worth and abilities. Each of us has developed a way of interpreting and explaining the business world around us. It's important that our stories neither damage us nor free us from blame. We should continue to feel worthy, accountable, and capable, with a mindset that allows us to continue to follow our entrepreneurial passion.[76]

3. If you don't have kind words to say about another person, say nothing. <u>Focus your energy around helping others versus tearing others down.</u> Dad advises, "Don't talk about the guy at the bar unless you want him talking about you."

"The Advantages of Positive Feedback" states that "Providing positive feedback encourages wanted behaviors. Perhaps the most straightforward advantage of positive reinforcement is that it directly fosters behaviors that a manager or business owner wants employees to repeat. Employees often suffer under a haze of uncertainty about what the exact expectations of a given position are. Negative feedback only inhibits the communication of what behaviors are expected within a role." [77]

FOR REFLECTION

"People will forget what you said. They will forget what you did. But they will never forget how you made them feel." — Maya Angelou

DO YOU TREAT EVERYONE WITH DIGNITY AND RESPECT? WHAT'S NEEDED FOR YOU TO BE MORE CONSIDERATE AS YOU DEAL WITH EMPLOYEES, CUSTOMERS, AND CLIENTS?

PUT INTO PRACTICE

HAVE YOU SAID THANK YOU RECENTLY WHEN SOMEONE DOES A GREAT JOB?

In the article "Five Thank You Notes Ever Entrepreneur Should Write," writer Amy Morin reveals "It takes humility and a sense of vulnerability to reach out to someone to say, "Thank you for what you've done for me." Daring to take this bold step, however, can be well worth the effort. Affirming how someone has made a difference in your life is one of the best gifts you could ever give someone."[78]

CHAPTER SEVENTEEN

Stretch Goals Push Us Forward

"You miss 100 percent of the shots you
don't take." —Wayne Gretzky

Jane was a friend of mine who was in a running club. Previously Jane had achieved success with local races. Now, she decided to set her aspirations on the goal of running in the Boston Marathon. Jane knew that to qualify for participation in the Boston Marathon; she would have to train very hard and be extremely disciplined.

Jane had not run this type of distance before, and now she endeavored to accomplish her goal through structured training techniques.

First, Jane set realistic distances to run. Once she achieved a short-term milestone, she established a new running target for herself. Jane trained for about eight months to prepare for the Boston Marathon and finished the race in excellent time.

PUT IT PRACTICE

"Setting goals is the first step in turning the invisible into the visible." —Tony Robbins

Establish mini goals with a more significant purpose in mind. Think of a stepping ladder. You climb every step, or at least a few steps at a time to reach the top of the ladder. Establishing realistic goals is essential. As well, it is helpful to challenge yourself to aspire to achieve far-reaching goals.

JANE'S THREEFOLD PRINCIPLES

Jane pushed herself to reach the ultimate goal. She understood that the disciple and tenacity were both attributes of success.

1. Establish a bigger goal for yourself or a "stretch goal." Push yourself to your next level.

2. Set a target for a "mini-milestone." Celebrate smaller wins that encourage you up to reach for the bigger goal.

3. Practice makes perfect. If you want to achieve a goal, you must be willing to put forth the effort to reach it.

Jane communicated, "I was turning forty. I felt that I had achieved success in many aspects of life, yet the goal of running the Boston Marathon was a stretch goal for me. I had to be tenacious in training and use my mind to visualize myself finishing the race. I had a mindset of no excuses on days when I didn't feel like putting forth the effort. On those days, I had to push myself to envision the end goal. Along the way, I set and achieved mini-targets which gave me the confidence to work towards a bigger goal."

FOR REFLECTION

DO YOU CELEBRATE MINI-GOALS ALONG THE WAY THAT HELPS YOU OR YOUR TEAM ACHIEVE THE BIGGER ASPIRATION?

In "Celebrate Milestone Successes to Maintain a Positive Work Environment" it is suggested that "Regularly celebrating with employees the accomplishment of short and long-term goals can be very motivating for them. Spontaneous celebrations with an element of surprise are always received well and create a spirit of camaraderie." [79]

CHAPTER EIGHTEEN

Gratitude is Attitude

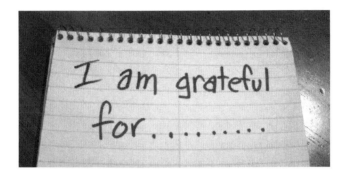

"When I started counting my blessings, my
whole life turned around." — Willie Nelson

What if you celebrate the good things in life, and
wake up each day with a feeling of appreciation for life's
blessing? Try to complete each day with remarks of
gratitude.

You may forget to acknowledge or give thanks for the
simple aspects of life that are of great value, such as, a
safe environment to live in, clean water to shower with,
food on the table, healthy children, or an employee who
lands a sales contract that translates into prosperity for
your business.

Elle Russ, best selling author of *The Paleo Thyroid
Solution* shares, "Before getting out of bed, I take a few
minutes to stretch under the covers and *express gratitude* for my body and health. I set an intention for the

day, and I usually say it to myself out loud. I drink a full glass of water, make coffee or tea, light candles, and daydream while setting more intentions about my goals." [80]

CASE EXAMPLE: SHIFTING MINDSET TOWARDS GRATITUDE

Recently a college friend who is a successful business person contacted me for a meetup. Before getting together, I asked, "how he was doing?" And he proceeded to share everything that wasn't working in his life including the lack of personal time for a run, and the constant struggle to create any time for himself.

I listened with an open heart to the conversation, but I felt agitated with everything he stated about what wasn't working right in life.

I responded, "Wouldn't it be nice to appreciate what is going right in life versus focusing on the aspects of life that you feel isn't working? What do you feel is necessary to make an immediate shift in your mindset?"

My friend was silent, so I asked the same question again, then continued, "Stop focusing on what is not working in life! Focus your energy on honoring yourself for what is going well."

I can recall many conversations as a flashback with other entrepreneurs who complain about how their customer doesn't value them, or how they feel stuck in life. There is often a feeling of lack instead of recognition for the good things in life. The emphasis is on the glass-half-empty instead of being half-full.

WHY EXPRESSING GRATITUDE CAN HELP YOU

In "Six Tips to Master Your Internal Dialogue," Adam Brady reveals "Gratitude is a powerful mental state that causes a palpable transformation in our internal landscape. When we put our attention on those things we can be grateful for, it automatically shifts us out of a negative mentality. Just by simply repeating the statement, I am so grateful for ____; we create positive momentum in our internal dialogue." [81]

At some point, I followed up with my college friend who initially saw life from the viewpoint of lack versus abundance. He surprised me by saying, "I appreciated your candidness during our last conversation. It helped me notice that I was spending too much energy focusing on what wasn't working in life. I immediately listened to a podcast about claiming one's destiny, and that helped me get back on track. I was able to shift my attention to focus on the positive aspects of life. I then opened a notebook and wrote down five things that I am grateful for in life."

I could tell by his voice that great things were in store for him. He committed himself to place attention on those things that made him happy. Moreover, he made a conscious choice to express gratitude.

As I recollect our conversation here, I can't help but wonder, "What if you were to express gratitude each day for the blessings in your life?"

CURIOUS ABOUT THE CONCEPT OF GRATITUDE, I POSED THE FOLLOWING QUESTION TO MY FACEBOOK NETWORK: **I AM GRATEFUL FOR?**

The response to this question was interesting. Friends, readers, and colleagues published responses ranging from being grateful for such things as their breath, the wind, and sunsets, to moments spent with an aging parent, hugs exchanged with their children, walks with their dog, growing a garden, amazing clients, and trips taken with their families.

"Why Entrepreneurs Need to Practice Gratitude every day" offers the following advice, "Like any mental discipline, gratitude takes times and practice. Still, if you commit to a daily practice, you'll see the benefits in your life. You'll be a happier and more fulfilled person, a more efficient and less emotional leader, and a better resource for your customers."[82]

PUT INTO PRACTICE

A gratitude journal can offer you a place to chronicle things and define aspects of your life that you are grateful on a daily basis. Robert Emmons, a leading gratitude researcher, has conducted multiple studies on the link between gratitude and well-being. His studies confirm that gratitude effectively increases happiness and reduces depression.

CHAPTER NINETEEN

Everybody Needs a Cheerleader

"None of us is as smart as all of us." —Kenneth H. Blanchard

Why are you so afraid to ask for help from others? You might be preconditioned to think that asking for help means weakness, but that notion couldn't be further from the truth. Seek guidance and advice from successful entrepreneurs who can advance your skills without you having to learn by extensive experience. [83]

Every person can benefit from a guide who provides insight. Instead, many people elect to sail solo thinking it's best to tackle most things independently. Conversely, there is a great, collective spirit in engaging others to support you.

"I always saw the value of pulling in others with key talents and leveraging their knowledge." —Mary, a former colleague.

"In my corporate job, we had to partner with other departments to get projects done. When I became an Entrepreneur, I felt like I operated in a silo. Later, I realized that cross partnership could collectively help all of our businesses." — David, an entrepreneur.

IT TAKES A VILLAGE- TEAMWORK

They say it takes a village to build a community. One person can't do everything. Collaboration and strategic partnerships that are mutually beneficial to everyone is a brilliant idea for entrepreneurs.

When celebrity stylist, Thom Filicia released his first book, "Thom Filicia Style" I was contacted by his business manager, who asked, "Are you available to host Thom's hometown book launch, can you help with publicity to make the event a success?".

Around the same time, Thom appeared on *The Oprah Winfrey Show*. Thom was familiar with the "national stage" format. Therefore, the pressure was on me to produce an event that was on par with his expectations. Because of the aggressive timelines needed to create, promote and deploy the evening's activities, the amount of work appeared daunting.

To ensure success, I created a list of potential partners. I reached out to the local independent bookstore to arrange for them to handle the book sales at the event. I rang the local hair salon, Bijou, a local woman-owned business, and they agreed to sell tickets for the event at the hair salon. This decision was strategic as hair salons are a vital point of connection with any local community.

I hired a friend who is excellent at staging events to help me effectively use the space. I phoned the Director of Alumni Affairs at Thom's alma mater, Syracuse University, and asked if they want to participate in the forum. They end up being very excited to join in the community-based event.

Finally, I contacted a local nonprofit organization, Positive Pink Packages to help spread the word about ticket sales given that the evening proceeds would provide breast cancer diagnosis packages, offered in honor of Thom's mother. At that point, we connected with the local television station to feature the event. Given, I was a member of women helping women organization; I networked with this extensive network to help with sponsor and vendor ideas.

The night was a smashing success. The community united and worked together, and I was incredibly grateful for the fantastic partners who made the evening an incredible achievement.

Thom Filicia and me at a subsequent event where he also donated book proceeds.

IDEAS FOR COLLABORATIVE EFFORTS AND CROSS PARTNERSHIP

Seek out people to partner within your community. Collaborate regarding events, product launches, and open houses that will be mutually beneficial. Several important partnerships may exist as possibilities for fundraising events, product launches, and business openings in your communities. Explore all your options. Contact the local chamber of commerce, rotary clubs, church groups, or business roundtables and explore what opportunities exist for collaborative partnerships.

"Five Smart Ways to Integrate Cross Promotion with Online Marketing" defines cross-promotion as "a technique whereby you utilize another medium or channel to promote or distribute services and products to new markets. It is a powerful and inexpensive approach to generate more sales and expand marketing efforts. In simple words, you find a partner that sells a complementary product to your company, and you cross-promote each other."

"Don't be shy about reaching out to contacts in a network. The worse they can say is "no thank you," and you will never hear a "yes unless you ask."[84]

CHAPTER TWENTY

Customers Expect Us to Get It Right

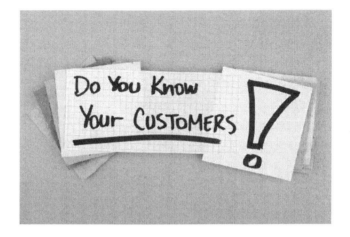

"If you do build a great experience, customers tell each other about that. Word of mouth is very powerful." — Jeff Bezos[85]

Customers are our bread and butter. They help us pay the bills. Over time, customers turn out to be our friends, champions or our worst nightmares. It is essential in engaging with a customer that you have a clear understanding of the dynamic of the relationship. Establish expectations of services at the time they hire your company's services. Customers will often make assumptions if you do not take the necessary time to build a relationship based on trust.

POINT TO PONDER AND PUT INTO PRACTICE

"Don't try to tell the customer what he wants. If you want to be smart, be smart in the shower. Then get out, go to work, and serve the customer!"[86]
— Gene Buckley

It is always better to ask the customer for input instead of assuming you know the answer. The article "Why Entrepreneurs Need to Be Good Listeners" indicates that "Listening to someone's opinion means you are respecting them and their thoughts, and that you care for them. You can read the full article at https://yourstory.com/2016/10/develop-good-listening-skills[87]

FOR REFLECTION

ARE YOU IN TUNE WITH WHAT CUSTOMERS THINK ABOUT YOUR PRODUCTS AND SERVICES?

"No matter how many customers you have, each is an individual. The day you start thinking of them as this amorphous 'collection' and stop thinking of them as people is the day you start going out of business."— Dharmesh Shah, Co-Founder of HubSpot [88]

Remember not everyone will be a customer. You can weed out the prospects that aren't a good match. People have different likes and preferences. The more you understand your demographic, the easier to target potential customers, plus offer enhanced product offerings.

In the article "Determining Your Ideal Customer," the following advice is offered: "Determine the specific benefits your customer is seeking in buying your product. Of all the benefits you offer, which are the most important to your ideal customer? What are the most pressing needs that your product or service satisfies? Why should your customer buy from you rather than from someone else?"[89]

A POSITIVE CUSTOMER EXPERIENCE ENTAILS AN OCCURRENCE THAT YOU WANT TO TELL YOUR FRIENDS ABOUT

"Treat the customer like you would want to be treated. Period!" —Brad Schweig

I met Frank at the local BMW dealership. He was Italian, had silver fox gray hair and played in a rock band. I liked his energy from our first conversation. He welcomed customers with a spirit of kindness and offered me a cup of coffee.

Frank was in customer service and sales at the BMW dealership. While it may be his job to interact with customers, he went the extra mile for each customer, time and time again! Frank thanked me for taking my car to the BMW service department at the dealership. He established expectations upfront regarding the length of time to expect for the service appointment and presented me with a loaner car.

One might say, "Well that is his job!" However, a customer can tell if an employee goes the extra mile and Frank went above and beyond the call of duty for his customers.

According to <u>McKinsey study</u>, seventy percent of buying experiences are based on how the customer feels they're being treated.[90]

When I returned to pick up the car and turned in the loaner car, I presented Frank with a thank you gift, a bottle of his favorite wine. A simple gesture of appreciation like this went a long way.

Fast forward to eight months later when the car required service again. When I called to schedule the appointment, the customer service agent stated, "No loaner cards are available. You can expect the service appointment to be at least half of a day, if not longer."

Entrepreneurs are busy people. No one wants to sit at a dealership for hours. We want to quickly get in and out of doctor appointments, car appointments, and the grocery shopping because there is a list of significant things to complete. Our time is valuable.

When I arrived at the dealership this second time, Frank appeared and said, "I happened to notice your name on the work order, so I put a loaner car aside for you." I was ecstatic. What exceptional customer service! Frank was proactive and took the initiative to secure a loaner car.

Going the extra mile helps you to be more successful in everything you do, this is especially true in business. A study done by Marketing Donut found that only two percent of sales occur at a first meeting, which means ninety-eight percent of the time you are going to have to put in some extra time and effort to make a sale or close a deal. You need to stimulate interest, transition interest, share a vision and most importantly, go the extra mile to manage and develop that vision. [91]

TEN REASONS WHY CUSTOMER SERVICE IS YOUR MOST IMPORTANT METRIC

On average, it costs approximately five times more to attract a new customer to your business than is required to retain an existing customer. That logic on its own should highlight the importance of providing excellent customer service. [92]

Everyone loved Bob as their manager. He took the time to value his customers and employees. That's why he was a role model for many of the sales force. As a coach, I tend to notice behavior. One of the best practices that made an immediate impact on Bob's team was the penning of a five-minute thank you card.

Bob took the time on the first Friday of the month, to write his employees and customers. He wrote personal notes, not emails, and mailed the cards, with his signature. Because we live in a technologically driven world, people now expect emails or instant messages. The fact that Bob penned a note by hand translated into more business referrals and job satisfaction among his employees.

Bob wasn't general in his thank you notes either, he would directly tell the employee or customer why they made a positive impact on him, or the company or he might praise the person for their contribution. The simple act of a thank-you card goes a long way.

CHAPTER TWENTY-ONE

What Low-Flying Planes Showcase about the Importance of Communication

"Good communication is as stimulating as black coffee, and just as hard to sleep after." — Anne Morrow Lindenberg

Recently, I returned home from a visit with my family members who live near Buffalo, New York. When I arrived home, I immediately noticed that outside the house there was a large sign that said, "Low Flying Planes." As it was not there before my travel, I thought to myself, "Where did this sign come from?".

My house is historic having been built in 1898. Across the street from the house is the local airport. The airport is a safe distance from my home and has plenty of green grass available for placement of the "Low Flying Plane" sign.

I rang the neighbor who lives adjacent to me. I am fortunate to have wonderful neighbors. During our discussion, I was informed that there is a property easement that extends about eight feet from the road to the property line, and the town owns the easement.

I saw that an arrow was spray-painted from the paved road across the stretch of easement towards where the Low Flying plane sign was cemented into the ground. Therefore, the town highway department had come onto my property to measure and ensure the distance was within the legal range for an easement. Not one person had bothered to notify me that a sign or an easement would be placed on the land. I have lived on my property for six years, and there hasn't ever been a sign, so I was upset!

I wondered why no one thought enough to contact me to discuss the sign's placement respectfully. Am I supposed to be okay with this lack of communication?

The placement of the sign could have been on across on the street at the airport's property. A trusted contractor suggested that I extract the sign and move it there. I contemplated this action; instead, I saw the experience as a lesson in the importance of communication among several people with varying points of view on the same subject.

Bestselling author Brian Tracy conveys, "Communication is a skill that you can learn. It's like riding a bicycle or typing. If you're willing to work at it, you can rapidly improve the quality of every part of your life."[93]

ENTREPRENEURS FORGET THAT A CRITICAL INGREDIENT TO COMMUNICATION IS A TWO-WAY CONVERSATION.

"I speak to everyone in the same way, whether it is the garbage man or the President of the University."
—Albert Einstein

At times, you may make decisions without engaging customer input or seeking employee perspectives. Many business owners communicate ineffectively. Employees don't want to arrive at work and hear from their co-worker as opposed to their supervisor about critical policy changes or newly established ways of doing business.

Employees want to be part of the company's operational dialogue. They want to offer input and feel their voice matters. In your role as a business owner, it is vital to involve constituents, employees, and customers in how your business will be run.

The Society for Human Resource Management offers, "Engaged employees are satisfied with their jobs, enjoy their work and the organization, believe that their job is important, take pride in their company, and believe that their employer values their contributions. One study found that highly engaged employees were five times less likely to quit than employees who were not engaged."[94]

When you sacrifice communication with employees or customers, they cannot expect a joyful response! Frustration may lead to employee turnover or a reduction in customer retention. Communication builds trust. Customers value honest and open conversations. They notice if a manager or organization is "walking the talk." Employees share comments about their workplace. The last thing you want to hear is that you mistreated employees.

The Gallup Poll found that consistent communication whether done in person, over the phone or electronically, is connected to higher human engagement. For example, employees whose managers hold regular meetings with them are almost three times as likely to be engaged as employees whose managers do not hold regular meetings with them. [95]

FOR REFLECTION

"People are the most important thing. Business model and product will follow if you have the right people." —Adam Neumann, Co-founder of We Work [96]

DO YOU COMMUNICATE ON A REGULAR BASIS WITH STAFF AND CUSTOMERS? DO YOU SOLICIT THEIR INPUT? HOW CAN YOU IMPROVE YOUR COMMUNICATION TECHNIQUES?

"We were caught up in the act of delivering goods to customers. So, we stopped having weekly staff meetings since our focus was on order fulfillment. That was a mistake because the connection to each other as a team was a critical success element. In hindsight, when we lost   employees, we knew it was because we lacked the commitment to involved employees in every step of the process." — Sharon, a customer service provider.

CHAPTER TWENTY-TWO

Vision to See into the Future

"A strong visual imagination acts as a
magnet to draw the visualized into
reality." — Anupama Garg

Vision is the vital energy that drives the entrepreneur, the founder, the co-founder, and his immediate team. Vision is what makes them dare: dare to explore, dare to challenge, dare to insist, dare to keep pushing, dare to have the determination to succeed. Vision is the energy that provides an entrepreneur and its organization with the ability to perform and succeed.[97]

It's essential for a vision to strike a balance between being highly imaginative and realistic. A vision represents "bigger-picture" aspirations, not just a set of practical objectives.98

"I couldn't see what was in front of me. I was too caught up in the day-to-day operations of the business and didn't have time to plan. In hindsight, I wish I would have spent, more time envisioning and dreaming about where the business could go and put a plan in place to realize the vision." — anonymous entrepreneur

FOR REFLECTION

DO YOU SPEND TIME DREAMING ABOUT THE FUTURE? DO YOU HAVE A ROADMAP OR ASPECTS TO A PLAN IN PLACE TO SUPPORT THE VISION? DO YOU HAVE A VISUAL OF YOUR GOAL OR DREAM?

TAKE ONE STEP TO PUT A VISION IN PLACE

Inspiration can arrive at the most unusual of times. Creativity cannot be constrained to a designated period or a certain hour of the day. As you ponder about your dream or vision, it is beneficial to hold in your mind a visual of the idea.

About six years ago, I participated in a class on creating vision boards. The instructor, Pamela Moss, utilized creativity planning sessions as an impetus to help others create a visual of their dreams. During the sessions, class participants placed images and words on a poster board set on an easel, to create a pictorial of ideas. In my case, I choose pictures of gardens, book covers, places I wanted to travel to, and various other photographs that spoke to me.

I then wrote category titles on the poster board to include: "Community," "Bestselling," "Abundance," and "Peace." These words represented my interpretation of some of the images on the vision board. I left the planning session with a graphic of my vision, a future pictorial of things that I wanted to create in life and work. When I arrived home, I hung the vision board on the closet door in my office, since I frequently open that door.

I made a conscious choice to spend time viewing the poster board visual from my office desk chair and permitted myself time to feel the emotion of my vision conjured. Since then, many of the vision board items have become realities. I believe it was more than creating a picture of the vision; accessed how the vision might feel if it was realized, all the while ensuring I was not attached to any outcome.

Today, in the workshops I teach for bestselling authors and entrepreneurs, we start with a blank canvas and create what are called "dream wheels." Dream wheels are images of the dreams that we hold for ourselves. The detailed dreams/future pictorials unfold in greater detail after we do a group kick-off exercise to harmonize everyone's energy and ignite creativity.

At the top of the dream wheel is one question: "My biggest dream is?'" and within two hours, a pictorial exists of the dream. The process then involves defining mini-goals to support the bigger vision. We can hold the biggest hopes for ourselves, although to manifest desired outcomes, we need to take many steps towards the implementation, towards the bigger vision.

New York Times author, Jack Canfield offered this advice on his blog called "Vision Board Ideas and How to Make Yourself Better," "Also known as dream boards, these simple devices are one of the most valuable visualization tools available to you. The inspirational collages serve as your image of the future – a tangible example, idea or representation of where you are going. They should represent your dreams, your goals, and your ideal life." [99]

THE DREAM JAR

You may not have the time to attend a vision board class but what you can do is place a visual that serves as a motivational tool for you in some location where you frequently view the image. One idea is to tape up pictures on your refrigerator and encourage your family to do the same as creators of your collective dream. Then engage as a family by spending time talking and sharing your feelings about the dream taking one action step towards the goal.

Another suggestion is to label a jar, "Dream Jar" with more specific markings such as "Personal Vacation" or "Family Trip." Over time, you and your family members can add money to the Dream Jar, as well as, decorate the jar with printed images representing the dream.

Author Tina Naughton Powers said, "Vision boards can provide us with a blueprint that aligns our desires with reality. Through the images and words, we choose, we become inspired to move forward with ideas for the future we might never have considered before."[100]

CHAPTER TWENTY-THREE

You have the Ability for Greatness

"All power is within you. You can do anything and everything."
— Swami Vivekananda

What if your wildest dream could finally become a reality? Within your genetic makeup is DNA coding that hosts your talents, likes, dislikes, and preferences. Once you awaken the part of you that knows your passionate purpose, there is no holding you back. What happens to many of us, however, is that we tend to live in a dormant mental state and lack commitment needed for self-discovery.

When you connect with truest yourself, you recognize intuitive feelings, sensations, and or gut reactions. Your inner compass becomes a directional tool for life's roadmap. Slowing down and staying mentally present helps you operate from a place of balance.

Evolved entrepreneurs (those who have mastered self-awareness) aren't afraid to push themselves to new heights of awareness. They set goals and keep raising the bar on their potential. They don't want to become stagnant, so they keep evolving. They see the capacity for business growth, new ventures, and employee development; they operate from a space that yields the best outcome for everyone.

When you are in alignment with your highest potential, boundless possibilities exist, and all countless things become viable. Whatever your dream is, you shed any limited beliefs that hold you back and claim your ability to manifest deep desires. As you establish goals, you learn that the achievement of mini-goals provides confidence and reassurance that you are on the right path.

I remember one of my dreams was to vacation at the ocean. Whenever a longing to fulfill this dream emerged, I closed my eyes and sensed the sea. I tasted the salty sea air. I sifted grains of the sand between my toes. I held a starfish in my hand. I felt the sun's warmth on my shoulders. In these moments, a part of me transcended time and space. I saw figures around me, silhouettes of people, whose faces I couldn't make out. This visual felt very real to me.

I knew that I desired to go to the sea. I wasn't clear who I would meet there, yet the simple sense that I would be at the ocean was my predominant thought.

After two years of visualizing, I taught a transformational retreat at Turks and Caicos. A client had arranged the venue. As I look back now, I see the synchronicity and believe that all mental paths on some level connected. My teaching at the retreat near the sea represented the power of the mind!

FOR REFLECTION

"If you can't fly then run if you can't run then walk if you can't walk then crawl, but whatever you do you have to keep moving forward." —Martin Luther King Jr.

You create experiences every day. And experiences happen which cause you to take notice, whether the occurrence is synchronicity or just coincidence. Either way, the message is to permit yourself to dream. Then define the actions steps, or at least one explicit action step forward. In the process, feel the dream as if it is your current truth.

PUT INTO PRACTICE

HOW CAN YOU BE MINDFUL OF TAKING TIME TO PAUSE TO OBTAIN CLARITY OF MIND? AND UTILIZE YOUR INNER WISDOM TO HELP YOU ACHIEVE YOUR GOALS AND DREAMS?

CHAPTER TWENTY-FOUR

Just Richard and The Rainbow

"Somewhere over the rainbow, the skies are blue, and the
dreams that you dare to dream
really do come true." — lyrics to *Somewhere Over the
Rainbow*, from the film, *The Wizard of Oz*

My sister was still sleeping in the villa; I didn't want
to wake her. I appreciated her making the journey to
partake in the retreat especially since community
sharing isn't something she feels drawn toward. As a
leader, my sister exudes team collaboration, yet in
private moments, she likes to keep to herself. Life as a
mom is very hectic for her, and certainly, most anyone

would be inclined to want to relax when spending time in the Caribbean.

Once the retreat began, I would be in teacher mode. I think that was part of the anxiety I was feeling like when you are about to give a speech or sales pitch or do something that you precisely how to do, but somehow feel hesitant.

Anxiety can also be a mirror to feelings of excitement. I have learned that anticipation comes when trying new things once we step past fears of "what if?" we settle into knowing that everything is going to unfold as it should.

On the day of the retreat, I was hyper-cognizant of time. In the morning, I desired some quiet time to myself at the ocean. I set my alarm for 6:45 am and got dressed in striped colored yoga pants and a pink t-shirt. I poured myself a glass of water and ventured to the ocean, but despite my best efforts, I couldn't exit the villa because the door was stuck. After twenty-three minutes, I was finally able to open the door. As I left, I caught the time on the clock on the villa wall.

Once outside the villa, I walked at a fast pace down a gravel path with palm trees. The sky was a tad murky; nonetheless, I felt sunshine would emerge shortly. Despite the morning's cloudiness, the infinity pool I passed seemed to exuded brilliance. It almost made me want to dive deep into the pool. Instead, I continued to the ocean. For two days prior, I had walked to the left of the hotel on the beach, yet for whatever reason, at the moment, I decided to venture to the right.

I was fully prepared regarding the content to teach at the retreat, yet a restlessness kept coming to the surface with the reoccurring question: "What do the people desire that will offer meaning in their lives?"

The universe has a hysterical sense of humor. As I pondered this question, I intersected with a man named "Just Richard." He appeared out of nowhere. I wasn't even aware of his presence at first.

Just Richard had wavy brown hair that fell below his earlobes. Brown rimmed glasses covered a third of his face over his brown eyes. He was dressed in a plaid linen shirt with blue shorts, and his sandals were in his hand, as he stood with his feet planted in the ocean sand.

"Good day for a rainbow!" he shouted.

At first, I didn't think I heard him. He could have been yelling to anyone. But on this particular day, there were very few people on the beach.

He yelled again and said "Hey, I am talking to you. Good day for a rainbow."

I thought, who says that?

He continued to bark out, "Would you like a rainbow today?"

"Sure!" I thought, who wouldn't love a colorful rainbow. Life doesn't work that way, most times we are rooted in the mud of conflict with ourselves or trying to run our businesses while mustering up a speckle of energy for personal matters.

Before I knew it, Just Richard was standing next to me with his feet lodged in the sand, when he asked, "What if you had all the money in the world?"

Before I could respond, he continued, "Instead of sitting on the beach relaxing, you ponder the meaning of your life. You know that money can't buy you happiness. Money can't buy you health. Money is only a vehicle to get you to have the best seat at the theater, but then the curtain closes, and you wonder what follows for you in life. I'm Just Richard. And you are?"

The conversation felt very unusual. There was a deep sense of a soul connection as Richard looked straight into my hazel eyes with such conviction. I sensed a familiarity, but I had never met this man before. Before I could utter a word, Richard asked, "What are you doing here? You know your words have meaning."

I finally responded, and there seemed to be a certain eloquence in my response, "I am here to teach retreat participants. I spoke an intention to the ocean before I met you. I wanted to know what to teach the people today. I wrote out a speech; still, I feel a deeper message exists that I am supposed to communicate."

Richard kicked the sand under his feet, stepped closer to me and exclaimed, "Nothing that you have prepared for today will go as you think. Tell your students to be present. Give them the tools to be closer to themselves, to appreciate the moments, and to lead others from a place of interconnection, love, and balance."

As entrepreneurs, we value being appreciated and respected for the work performed. I wondered how I was supposed to tell people to place love into their businesses, and how this message would be received among a group of notably logic-minded professionals.

Richard must have sensed from my body language that I was hesitant about the insight he presented, so he rephrased his thoughts, "Tell them they need an interconnection with themselves. To lead anyone, they need first to understand themselves. Only then can they do the work they are capable of doing. You know that people will follow a leader who has the heart to elevate them while also championing self-discovery. That is your role, to awaken them."

Then he pointed to the sky and said, "I told you to expect rainbows."

In front of Just Richard and me was a rainbow with the most magnificent kaleidoscope of colors to include: red amber, purple, and yellow, a fusion of color. It looked like a painting in the sky.

Time seemed suspended in the moments that I observed the rainbows.

Richard and I bantered back and forth. He was adamant about people needing to awaken and form a connection with themselves. His viewpoints reminded me of what Arianna Huffington once said, "I wish I could go back and tell myself that not only is there no trade-off between living a well-rounded life and high performance is improved when our lives include time for renewal, wisdom, wonder, and giving. That would have saved me a lot of unnecessary stress, burnout, and exhaustion." [101]

In hindsight, I wondered if the universe staged me meeting Just Richard in response to my plea for wisdom regarding what I should impart to the retreat participants. I am a big believer in synchronicity. Either way, I am forever grateful for the sage guidance that Just Richard offered me.

After a short time, the rainbow began to fade away. At that moment, I closed my eyes and felt the sun on my face, and tasted the sea-salted air on my lips.

Before parting, Just Richard offered me some final words, "Pause and don't let life pass you. I've had money. I was the artist who always saw the finished painting before it was constructed. Nevertheless, don't lose sight of the present moment, for you may only have a few more to share with others."

The sand seemed to hold a holographic image of footprints, which must have been Richard's.

I have often reflected on Richard's views. I feel he was a gift that arrived exactly when the universe decided it would be best.

The clear message here is: you must take time to form an interconnection with yourself. That to be the best version of ourselves, to lead others, to be entrepreneurs, to make our contribution on this planet; we need to appreciate those moments that lead up to the possibility of a rainbow in the sky that serves as a hopeful symbol. In being present, we can listen to each other's needs and perspectives.

"In connecting with ourselves, we find peace and clarity, and we appreciate the gift of the moment as we move towards the future." — Just Richard

CHAPTER TWENTY-FIVE

Moving Forward

"Your dream is a reality that is waiting
for you to materialize. Today is a new
day! Don't let your history interfere with
your destiny! Learn from your past so
that it can empower your present and
propel you to greatness." — Steve
Maraboli

What a terrific ride it has been to arrive at this place
in time, and how magnetic it is to explore new ideas and
share my thoughts with you. Now it is time to put into
practice the concepts that have been presented. As an
entrepreneur, you are constantly adapting to the conditions in your environment. Life is fast moving; so, you
must make a conscious choice to slow down. Working

lists are good frameworks to follow to make progress, but you can become consumed by the details, and forget to see the vista in front of you.

Work is a significant part of our lives, therefore, let's make work fun. Employees want to work in fun places. Infuse creative pauses in the workday for your staff. I used to say, "I need a break from work." Instead, I now reaffirm, "I am taking a fifteen or thirty-minute creative pause." Can you see the shift in mindset? The word "break" sends a message out the universe that you need a break from work - using the word "pause" shifts your energy.

As you most likely juggle many tasks at once, you need to nourish *you!* The easiest way to fuel yourself is with contemplative practices, by eating healthily and drinking water. One of the greatest gifts you can acquire is a connection to yourself. When you tap inward and tune into your thoughts and emotions, you sense, feel and ignite ideas. An excavator excavates; you can discover and open the aspects of consciousness that live within you.

Be mindful of your thoughts. Thoughts can manifest into reality. You become what you believe about you. Hence, don't limit yourself with negative self-talk. Instead, expend your energy on positivity. Direct your awareness toward amplifiers such as vision planning, dreaming, and the power of intention. Believing what you feel will help you become an evolved entrepreneur.

If you tuck the *Entrepreneurial Compass* in the basement in a closet that rarely gets opened, it will sit there and collect dust until some occurrence forces you to open it. If you recognize that the compass is already within you, you can reach into your internal compass for clarity with decision making. When you center yourself like a compass, you operate from a space of balance.

Life is what you make it. Take time to enjoy an sunset or a sunrise. *You have one life to live, live it without regrets.* Learn what speaks to you in the adventure of life. Embrace experiences. Explore. Focus your energy on experiencing the things that make you happy.

Unleash the childlike wonder in you. Take risks. Don't hold yourself back by erroring on the side of caution.

Recognize the brilliance within you. Be all that you can be as a teacher, mentor, and creator. And never stop learning! In the article, "Why Every Entrepreneur Needs a Mentor," stresses the following notion: "A lot of people fail to recognize the true value of having someone to talk to or confide in, and it's a real shame because mentoring matters. It makes a difference; it can impact your business in very tangible ways."[102]

As you step forward to claim what you desire – know that you are capable of living the life of your dreams with joy, balance, and prosperity. You get to choose your experience, so, place your attention where you want to go and direct your efforts towards big dreams. Remember at the end of the day - take a few moments to inhale life's blessings and celebrate you!

Lakewood Speech Keynote Excerpt

Me with Gabrielle Jackson who is recognized at Lakewood's *Women Celebrating Women* event.

We have come together to celebrate our accomplishments. As I feel the excitement about sharing a collective consciousness with you, I recognize that we have more in common than our differences.

Sometimes, you forget to remember that in unison you are stronger than operating in a silo. You grow up in a world where a mindset of competition, working harder and achieving more are the pivotal qualities of success. But collaboration, teamwork, and mentorship are the pathway to advancing businesses and organizations.

As entrepreneurs, we can influence and empower each other and offer words of encouragement. In helping another, the universal laws of attraction will bring forth a reciprocal action. That is why you must be mindful of your words and movements. It is easy to lose sight of what is in front of you and neglect to see the value the precious moments of a day.

In the midst of leading a busy life, your attention can be split between doing and being. In spaces of "just being," you gain clarity, peace and contemplative time.

Self-belief rises to the surface. Determination follows as your authenticity emerges to support your choices. Then you are free to explore, dream and discover that which makes you happy.

I would like to close this book with a personal story

I experienced an identity crisis at age thirty-three. I was very good at my job, earned over 250,000 dollars annually, and had the persona of a high achiever. You could say I had reached a pinnacle of success. On the surface, I looked completely put together. Nonetheless, as each day passed, I was slowing losing a part of myself.

I was everything to everyone else, except for me. Instead of pausing long enough to notice that which was in front of me, I ran. I ran from the hotel where I traveled weekly to the corporate office. When I run, I obtain mental strength. I was running thru life entirely unaware that I needed to slow down long enough to be present to sense, feel and be part of life.

Then, one day, I had enough. It was time for a change. The restlessness within me was deepening. I couldn't shake the feeling that life could offer more. So, I left everything, a husband, a white picketed fence (literally), a steady paycheck, and a corporate job.

I started my consulting company and went to a conference in the industry with only a business card that I had designed four days before the summit. I landed my first client within twenty minutes. He was a CEO of his own company, and he had previously worked at the company which I left. Work-related trips to New York City began soon after that.

I substituted one vice for another vice. I leaped directly into consulting. Instead of taking time to explore the truth within me which was a longing for more flexibility and a desire to be genuinely passionate about the work I performed, I settled.

Fear of money held me back. I had become dependent on a lifestyle, and my income was providing me with financial stability. Until the day arrived, when I realized could no longer let money dictate my happiness. I had to find myself again and take a chance on discovering a passionate purpose.

I went to a wellness spa to recharge and seek clarity. I walked in the desert for many hours, searching for what you might say is the soul's purpose. I longed to form a deeper connection with my most authentic self but had rarely been quiet enough to achieve any such internal bond.

The desert experience was my first self-guided retreat. In the desert, I found solace. I'd link to think that that the voices of the desert wind spoke to me, yet mostly, there was only silence. What I did experience was a pause that offered me enough time to notice a cactus in bloom.

Throughout the years that followed that trip, I explored many dimensions within myself, wrote books, and learned how to live a life of balance. I started a global publishing company, and I was very good at connecting people, so stories found me. I never again had to pursue anything.

I began to see, feel, and sense my intuition. I saw the direct benefit of visualization and was able to learn the art of instant manifestation. I created fascinating experiences as I took time to meditate and develop an interconnection with myself. Creativity followed, and my ability to coach others expanded as the creative muse awakened within me.

In the midst of my dynamic journey to this place in time, I learned that self-care is critical for survival. If you are going to run a business at the frequencies you are capable of, you must water the well within you.

The great Sufi poet, Rumi, once said, *"Everything in the universe is within you. Ask all from yourself."*

Like the butterfly who needs a gestation period for nourishment, certain phases of growth are critical for evolution. We are like a butterfly. We need time to evolve and grow our wings. Then, we can showcase to the world the markings of our talents. Image the possibility of a field full of butterflies, fluttering their brilliance, and collectively helping each other soar.

Entrepreneurial Insight, Lessons, and Tips from My Experience and Seasoned Entrepreneurs

"If something is important enough, or you believe something is important enough, even if you are scared, you will keep going." —Elon Musk, CEO of Tesla Motors and SpaceX[103]

ACQUIRE A CHEERLEADER. EVERYONE NEEDS A CHAMPION TO SAY A GREAT JOB.

DITCH THE NAYSAYERS. "OBTAIN ONE OR TWO PEOPLE WHO CAN LIFT YOU, NOT TEAR YOU DOWN." – REAL ESTATE ENTREPRENEUR

DON'T WASTE ENERGY WORRYING ABOUT YESTERDAY. IF YOU FESTER OVER YESTERDAY, YOU WILL MISS WHAT IS GOING ON RIGHT NOW!

LET GO OF PAST MISTAKES. RECOGNIZE THE GIFT GARNISHED FROM THE EXPERIENCE. LET'S FACE IT; EVERYONE MAKES MISTAKES. YOU DON'T KNOW WHAT YOU DON'T KNOW.

TREAT OTHERS HOW YOU WANT TREATMENT. BE MINDFUL OF YOUR WORDS AND ACTIONS. BE KIND AND OFFER A LISTENING EAR.

TAP INTO INTUITION FOR DECISION MAKING. LISTEN TO YOUR INNER GUT FEELINGS. TRUST YOUR INNER WISDOM.

CELEBRATE MILESTONES. TAKE TIME TO CELEBRATE THE SMALLER WINS THAT LEAD TO BIGGER OBJECTIVES. EMPLOYEES WHO FEEL APPRECIATION AND A SENSE OF PRIDE IN THEIR WORK SHOW UP FOR WORK EXCITED TO BE THERE.

ASK THE CUSTOMER. THEN LISTEN TO CUSTOMER RESPONSES. ASK, HOW CAN OUR COMPANY MEET YOUR NEEDS?

SET CUSTOMER EXPECTATIONS UP FRONT. DON'T KEEP THE CUSTOMER GUESSING.

JOIN FORCES. COLLABORATE. THE BEST PARTNERSHIPS COMES FROM FOLKS WHO WORK IN DIVERSE INDUSTRIES AND SEE THE VALUE OF HELPING EACH OTHER.

KEEP AN EYE ON FINANCES. "MAKE SURE YOU UNDERSTAND HOW MUCH YOU NEED MONTHLY TO OPERATE. CREATE A PLAN TO EXCEED THAT IN REVENUE. IF POSSIBLE, KEEP CASH IN RESERVE IN CASE YOU NEED LIQUID CAPITAL." – FINANCIAL AND CAPITAL INVESTOR

MASSIVE ISN'T ALWAYS BETTER. MAINTAINING YOUR CURRENT SIZE WITH LASER BEAM FOCUS CAN BE A SMART IDEA. "WE DECIDED TO STAY TRUE TO OUR CUSTOMERS INSTEAD OF TOO MUCH DIVERSIFICATION."- CONSULTANT

DON'T LIMIT YOURSELF! "STEP THROUGH THE DOOR OF OPPORTUNITY. IF NOT, YOU WILL HAVE REGRETS." – SERVICE PROVIDER

SHOW UP AND BE A PARTICIPANT. "LEAD BY EXAMPLE. ASK STAFF FOR INPUT AND TRUST TALENTED STAFF TO EXECUTE."
– ORGANIZATIONAL LEADER

WALK AWAY FROM A PROSPECTIVE CLIENT IF NOT A GOOD FIT. "WE SACRIFICED VALUES FOR MONEY, AND THAT WAS THE BIGGEST ERROR. THE SITUATION ALMOST SUCKED THE LIFE OUT OF THE COMPANY." – ANONYMOUS ENTREPRENEUR

ESTABLISH A MISSION STATEMENT. BE IMPECCABLE WITH YOUR WORDS AND STAY TRUE TO YOUR MISSION.

SEE IT AND BELIEVE IT. "THE DREAM BOARD IS POSTED FOR EMPLOYEES AND STAFF TO SEE. IT IS A VISUAL OF WHAT EACH EMPLOYEE DREAMS FOR THEMSELVES. EVERY EMPLOYEE CAN HANG UP A DREAM IMAGE. WE ALSO PLACE A COMPOSITE VISUAL AS A GROUP." – TECH INNOVATOR

BE OPEN-MINDED. "DON'T BE FIXATED ON DOING THINGS A PARTICULAR WAY. YOU MIGHT BE SURPRISED HOW YOUNGER WORKERS ARE VERY GOOD AT OFFERING SOLUTIONS AND NEW PRODUCT IDEAS." - RETAIL STORE OWNER

TIME TO RECHARGE. REBOOT. "I WAS SITTING AT MY DESK WISHING I HAD TAKEN MORE TIME FOR ME, INSTEAD OF LETTING WORK CONSUME ME.

DON'T LET THIS HAPPEN TO YOU." – SALESFORCE LEADER

FOLLOW PASSION. EXPLORE DESIRES. "I WENT INTO THE FAMILY BUSINESS. IN HINDSIGHT, I ALWAYS LOVED TO PAINT. I WISH I WOULD HAVE WORKED AT AN ART GALLERY OR EXPLORED WHAT THIS COULD HAVE MEANT FOR ME." – ENTREPRENEUR WHOSE FAMILY OWNS A BUSINESS

COMMUNICATION IS ESSENTIAL FOR SUCCESS. DON'T COMMUNICATE IN A SILO OR YOU WILL LOSE GOOD EMPLOYEES AND GREAT CUSTOMERS.

MAKE HEALTHY CHOICES. "MAKE A CONSCIOUS CHOICE TO TAKE TIME DAILY FOR YOU. IT IS INCREDIBLE HOW EASY IT IS TO ALWAYS HAVE A BOTTLE OF WATER WITH ME; IT IS A COMFORTABLE WAY TO STAY HYDRATED. DURING THE SUMMER MONTHS, I DROP IN FROZEN BLUEBERRIES OR RASPBERRIES IN WATER." – WELLNESS COACH AND ENTREPRENEUR

CREATIVITY EXPANDS. "THE BEST IDEAS I HAVE COME RIGHT AFTER MEDITATION OR IMAGINATION EXERCISES. CREATIVITY FLOWS, AND IDEAS POUR OUT OF ME." – MINDFULNESS TEACHER AND ENTREPRENEUR

CARVE OUT BREATHERS. "BREATHE. TODAY, I SIT IN A CAR FOR FIVE MINUTES, WINDOW OPEN AND BREATHE. I SEE MYSELF DROPPING WORRIES OFF MY SHOULDERS. I SEE GOLDEN LIGHT FILLING UP MY BODY." – LIFE COACH ENTREPRENEUR

JOINTLY SET INTENTIONS AT THE ONSET OF MEETINGS. "WE HAVE A TIBETAN BOWL. THE BOWL RINGS AT THE START OF MEETINGS. THE RINGING OF THE BELL SIGNIFIES FOR US TO COME TOGETHER. THEN STAFF WRITE ON THE WHITEBOARD - A COMMON INTENTION FOR THE MEETING." – ENTREPRENEURIAL COACH

BE PRESENT IN A CONVERSATION. "DID YOU EVER FORGET WHAT IS SAID BECAUSE YOUR MIND RACES TO THE FOLLOWING TASK? I DID, TOO MANY TIMES!" – SALLY, BUSINESS WOMAN AND MOM

RESILIENCE IS CRITICAL FOR ENTREPRENEURS. "YOU NEED TO KEEP SHOWING UP. QUOTES ON MY DESK AND A PICTURE OF MY KIDS ARE THE MOTIVATION ON WORKING DAYS WHEN TIMES GET TOUGH." – RETAIL STORE OWNER

BE MINDFUL OF WHAT YOU THINK. "MAN, THAT STUFF THAT LEAKS INTO THE SUBCONSCIOUS CAN MESS WITH SUCCESS. BE AWARE OF THOSE NEGATIVE TAPES. FOCUS ON THE POSITIVE STUFF." – FORMER CLIENT

LITTLE THINGS ADD UP TO BIGGER THINGS. SAY THANK YOU FOR A JOB WELL DONE. RECOGNIZE EVEN MINOR ACCOMPLISHMENTS SINCE VITAL TO SUCCESS IS HAPPY EMPLOYEES.

PLAYFULNESS – HAVE FUN AT WORK. "FOLKS THOUGHT WE WERE NUTS TO TAKE TIME OUT OF A WORKDAY TO GATHER EMPLOYEES FOR AN HOUR. NO WORK TALK, WE THROW DARTS, EAT CHICKEN WINGS AND PLAY A GAME OF CARDS.

THE EMPLOYEES CAN'T WAIT FOR CHICKEN WING FRIDAY." – FORMER CLIENT

STAY IN BALANCE."I LOST SIGHT OF EVERYTHING. MY HEALTH SUFFERED. I BARELY HELD ON TO MY FAMILY. MAKE SURE YOU MAKE TIME FOR FAMILY." – FINANCIAL PLANNER

START THE DAY WITH A MORNING ROUTINE. "I SIT MINDFULLY WITH A CUP OF COFFEE. AT THAT MOMENT, I SEE THE DAY AS UNFOLDING GREAT AND MEETING NEW PEOPLE WITH WONDERFUL EXPERIENCES." – WELLNESS ENTREPRENEUR

COMMUNITY ENGAGEMENT HELPS US GIVE BACK TO OTHERS. "IF YOU DON'T HELP EACH OTHER, WHO WILL HELP YOU WHEN YOU NEED IT MOST?" – ORGANIZATIONAL LEADER

Notes

1 "How to Discover and Unleash Your Strengths as an Entrepreneur," https://ryrob.com/discover-strengths-entrepreneur
2 "A Newbie Orienteer, And An Interview With Orienteering Canada,"https://kyraonthego.wordpress.com/2017/05/01/a-newbie-orienteer-and-an-interview

3 "Advantages of a Hand-Held GPS,"
http://handheldgpsinfo.com/advantages-of-handheld-gps/
4 Alex Jospe, The World Orienteering Club,
https://www.newenglandorienteering.org/o-articles/training
5 Brian Tracy, "Accessing Your Inner Guidance, Part One," https://www.briantracy.com/blog/personal-success/accessing-your-inner-guidance-part-one/
6 "Aligning Your Purpose and Passion Toward Entrepreneurship," https://bettercorp.nyc/events/2017/2/11/aligning-your-purpose-and-passion-towards-entrepreneurship
7 Sherie Campbell, "Seven Ways Entrepreneurs Can Master Self Awareness," https://www.entrepreneur.com/article/238754

8 "Time, An Entrepreneurs Most Valuable Resource," https://www.lockedownseo.com/time-entrepreneurs-most-valuable-resource/

9Richard Branson,https://www.virgin.com/entrepreneur/what-do-worlds-leading-entrepreneurs-do-their-time-others-dont
10 Melody Wilding, "Three Must Have Scripts for Saying No to Clients Nicely," https://melodywilding.com/3-must-have-scripts-for-saying-no-to-clients-nicely/
11 Entrepreneur.com, "Productivity Lifesaver: The 5-sentence Email - Entrepreneur,"
https://www.entrepreneur.com/article/226581
12 Vivian Nunez, Forbes.com, "How Having Big Dreams Can Help You As An Entrepreneur,
https://www.forbes.com/sites/viviannunez/2016/07/13/how-having-big-dreams-can-he

[13]Vivian Nunez, Forbes.com, "How Having Big Dreams Can Help You As An Entrepreneur, http://www.forbes.com/sites/viviannunez/2016/07/13/how-having-big-dreams-can-help-you-as-an-entrepreneur/

14 Richard Branson, "Why Dreaming Is So Important For...," https://www.virgin.com/entrepreneur/richard-branson-why-dreaming-so-important-en

15 Seattle Times, "J.K. Rowling Dreams She Is Harry Potter While Finishing...,"https://www.seattletimes.com/entertainment/jk-rowling-dreams-she-is-harry-potter

16 Gloria Steinmen, http://www.gloriasteinem.com/news/

17 Addictedtosuccess.com, "16 Reasons Why It's So Important To Follow Your Dreams", https://addicted2success.com/success-advice/16-reasons-why-its-important-to-foll

18 "Nine Reasons Entrepreneurs Take a Risk," http://www.majorkeymovements.com/9-reasons-entrepreneurs-take-risks-infographic/

19 The News Director's Office: Vera Jimenez, Ktla 5 News ..., https://ktla.com/2018/09/18/the-news-directors-office-vera-jimenez-ktla-5-news-m

20 The Australian Institute of Business, "Five Reasons Why Entrepreneurs Take a Risk," https://www.aib.edu.au/blog/entrepreneurship/5-reasons-entrepreneurs-take-risks/

21 "Invisalign - The Clear Choice" - Xiaxue.blogspot.com, http://xiaxue.blogspot.com/2010/11/invisalign-clear-choice.html

22 "Twenty Inspirational Quotes From Successful Entrepreneurs," https://activerain.com/blogsview/5269356/20-inspirational-quotes-from-successful

23 Center for Individualism.com, "Economic Opportunities Don't "exist". Entrepreneurs Create ...," https://www.centerforindividualism.org/economic-opportunities-dont-exist-entrepr

24 Tiny Buddha, "How To Let Go Of Negative, Limiting Beliefs About Yourself," https://tinybuddha.com/blog/how-let-go-negative-limiting-beliefs-about-yourself/

25 Andy Molinsky, Inc.com, "Want To Be A Successful Entrepreneur? Learn To Step ...," https://www.inc.com/andy-molinsky/want-to-be-a-successful-entrepreneur-learn-to-

26 Fortune.com, "Why Fear Makes You A Better Leader," http://fortune.com/2014/10/28/how-terrifying-challenges-make-better-leaders/

27 Entrepreneur.com, "10 Things You Can Do To Boost Self-confidence," https://www.entrepreneur.com/article/281874

28 "5 Roadblocks That Are Getting In The Way Of Your Business," https://www.entrepreneur.com/article/243421

29 Oswego County Today, News "Five Secrets To Create A Buzz Around Your Business Or ...," https://oswegocountytoday.com/five-secrets-to-create-a-buzz-around-your-business

30 Advancing Women.com, http://www.advancingwomen.com/entrepreneurialism/8777.php

31 Rebecca Kronman, "Mindfulness and Entrepreneurship: How Breathing Can Help Our Work," https://www.wework.com/creator/personal-profiles/mindfulness-and-entrepreneurship-how-breathing-can-help-our-work/

32 LionessesofAfrica.com, "Why Entrepreneurs Should Practice the Pause," http://www.lionessesofafrica.com/blog/2017/7/23/why-entrepreneurs-should-practice-the-pause

33 Successconsciousness.com, "How Many Thoughts Does Your Mind Think in One Hour," https://www.successconsciousness.com/blog/inner-peace/how-many-thoughts-does-your-mind-think-in-one-hour/

34 News Harvard University, "Wandering Mind Not a Happy Mind,"https://news.harvard.edu/gazette/story/2010/11/wandering-mind-not-a-happy-mind

35 Discovetheregion.com, "Can I Have A Can-do Attitude?" https://www.discovertheregion.com/can-can-attitude/

36 Pyschcentral.com, "7 Steps to Develop Awareness of Your Thoughts and Feelings", https://blogs.pyschcentral.com/relationship

37 Patel, Deepak, Entreprenuer.com, "Five Ways to Re Wire Your Brain to Be Positive," https://www.entrepreneur.com/article/296779

38 Entrepreneur.com, "The Extraordinary Power of Visualizing Success," https://www.entrepreneur.com/article/242373

39 Pyschmechanics.com, "Visualization Benefits And Its Impact On Motivation," https://www.psychmechanics.com/2014/11/visualization-benefits-and-its-impact.htm

40 Psychology Today, "Athletes Most Power Mental Tool, Psychology Today," https://www.psychologytoday.com/us/blog/the-power-prime/201211/sport-imagery-athletes-most-powerful-mental-tool

41 Entrepreneur.com, https://www.entrepreneur.com/article/232813

42 Theselfhelplibrary.com, "Positive Affirmations, Why Should We Practice Them," https://theselfhelplibrary.com/positive-affirmations-why-should-we-practice-them

43 Louise Hay, "The Power Of Affirmations" Official Website, https://www.louisehay.com/the-power-of-affirmations

44 Dr. Wayne W. Dyer, "Affirmation," https://www.drwaynedyer.com/blog/tag/affirmation

45 Morning Business Chat Blog,https://morningbusinesschat.com

46 Positivepyschologyprogram.com, "Daily Affirmations: Making Your Life Better One Day At A Time," https://positivepsychologyprogram.com/daily-affirmations

47 Entrepreneur.com, "Why Self-care Sometimes Needs To Be Your No. 1 Strategy," https://www.entrepreneur.com/article/271459

48 Sarah Vermut, Entrepreneur.com, "Why Self Care Needs to Be Your Number One Strategy," https://www.entrepreneur.com/article/271459

49 Men's Health Foundation Canada, "Men's Health Perceptions from Around the Globe," https://menshealthfoundation.ca/wp-content/uploads/2017/03/Men4Selfcare_Key.pdf

50 Lauren F Freidman, and Kevin Loria, Business Insider, " Eleven Scientific Reasons You Should Be Spending More Time Outside," https://www.businessinsider.com/scientific-benefits-of-nature-outdoors-2016-4

51 "3 Ways Being Present in The Moment Can Benefit Your Business," https://www.linkedin.com/pulse/3-ways-being-present-moment-can-benefit-your-business-ely-mba-cpc

52 Shannon Kaiser, *Find Your Happy: An Inspirational Guide To Loving Life To ...,* https://www.barnesandnoble.com/w/find-your-happy-shannon-kaiser/1113659242

53 Lifehack.org, "Ten Reasons Why Following Your Passion is More Important than Money," https://www.lifehack.org/articles/money/10-reasons-why-following-your-passion-more-important-than-money.html

54 Forbes.com, Mike Kappel, "Is Passion Good For Business?" https://www.forbes.com/sites/mikekappel/2017/02/22/is-passion-good-for-business/

55 https://www.whatsnext.com/5-tips-midlife-career-change/

56 Larry Kim, "Eight Skills Your Child Needs to Be the Next Great Entrepreneur," https://medium.com/the-mission/8-skills-your-child-needs-to-be-the-next-great-entrepreneur-99bd326d7c06

57 Oprah Winfrey, Oprah.com, "Your Energy Is Infinite And This Is Why",http://www.oprah.com/oprahs-lifeclass/your-energy-is-infinite-and-this-is-why/al

58 Business Daily News, "How To Harness Creativity As An Entrepreneur,"https://www.businessnewsdaily.com/5813-creativity-in-entrepreneurship.html

59 Cleverism Magazine, "Why Creativity Is So Crucial For Entrepreneurs?" https://www.cleverism.com/why-creativity-is-so-crucial-for-entrepreneurs/

56 SmallBizTrends.com, "20 Ways To Boost Your Entrepreneurial Creativity - Small ...," https://smallbiztrends.com/2015/02/boost-your-entrepreneurial-creativity.html

61 Entrepreneur.com, "10 Strategies For Overcoming Creativity Block - Entrepreneur,"
https://www.entrepreneur.com/article/230276

62 Business Daily News, "How To Harness Creativity As An Entrepreneur," https://www.businessnewsdaily.com/5813-creativity-in-entrepreneurship.html

63 Hubappirio.com, https://hub.appirio.com/careers-culture-blog/why-we-need-to-have-fun-at-work

64 Monster.com, "Why Fun At Work Matters,"
https://www.monster.com/career-advice/article/fun-at-work-matters-levity-effect

65 Psychology Today, "What Is Intuition, And How Do We Use It?"
https://www.psychologytoday.com/us/blog/the-intuitive-compass/201108/what-is-int

66 Science Daily, "Go With Your Gut - Intuition Is More Than Just A Hunch ...,"
https://www.sciencedaily.com/releases/2008/03/080305144210.htm

67 Psychology Today, "How To Use Your Intuition"
https://www.psychologytoday.com/us/blog/wander-woman/201409/how-use-your-intuiti

68 Huffington Post, "The 7 Attributes Of Intuitive Business Leaders,"https://www.huffingtonpost.com/simone-wright/business-intuition-what-d_b_5833396

69 Profit Management.com, "The Science Behind Intuitions ...,"
http://proffittmanagement.com/intuitions-theres-science-behind-them

70 Belinda Davidson, "Why Successful Business People Use Their Intuition," http://belindadavidson.com/why-all-successful-business-people-use-their-intuition

71 Psychology Today, "Resilience,"
https://www.psychologytoday.com/us/basics/resilience

[72] Gordon Tredgold, Inc.com, "Four Reasons Why Resilience is an Entrepreneurs Greatest Quality," https://www.inc.com/gordon-tredgold/4-reasons-why-entrepreneurs-need-to-be-resilient.html

[73] Entrepreneur.com, "Why Resilience is the Successful Quality for Entrepreneurship," https://www.entrepreneur.com/article/243910

[74] Huffington Post, "The Entrepreneurial Benefits of Being Selfless", https://www.huffingtonpost.com/anna-johansson/the-entrepreneurial-benef_b_9809254.html

[75] Entrepreneur.com, "Volunteering As A Benefit - Entrepreneur," https://www.entrepreneur.com/article/188360

[76] Forbes.com, "How To Increase Self-esteem And Success In Business," https://www.forbes.com/sites/martinzwilling/2014/01/23/how-to-increase-self-este

[77] Small Business Chronicle, "The Advantages of Positive Feedback,"https://smhttps://smallbusiness.chron.com/advantages-positive-feedback 18135.htmlallbusiness.chron.com/advantages-positive-feedback-18135.html

[78] Amy Morin, Forbes.com, "The Five Thank-you Notes Every Entrepreneur Should Write," https://www.forbes.com/sites/amymorin/2014/03/09/the-five-thank-you-notes-every-

[79] Entreprenuer.com, "Celebrate Milestone Successes To Maintain A Positive Work.," https://www.entrepreneur.com/article/273004

[80] Success.com, "10 Morning Routines of Wildly Successful Entrepreneurs," https://www.success.com/article/10-morning-routines-of-wildly-successful-entrepreneurs

[81] The Chopra Center, "6 Tips To Master Your Internal Dialogue," https://chopra.com/articles/6-tips-to-master-your-internal-dialogue

82 Chris Myers, Forbes.com, "Why Entrepreneurs Need To Practice Gratitude Each And.,"
https://www.forbes.com/sites/chrismyers/2018/03/21/why-entrepreneurs-need-to-pra

83 Forbes.com, "Why Entrepreneurs Need To Learn To Ask For Help,"https://www.forbes.com/sites/forbesagencycouncil/2016/07/27/why-entrepreneurs-ne

84 Entreprenuer.com, "5 Smart Ways To Integrate Cross-promotion With Online ...,"
https://www.entrepreneur.com/article/280211

85 Winthecustomer.com, "101 Best Inspirational Customer Service Quotes," http://winthecustomer.com/best-customer-service-quotes

86 Forbes.com, "40 Eye-opening Customer Service Quotes,"
https://www.forbes.com/sites/ekaterinawalter/2014/03/04/40-eye-opening-customer-

87 Yourstory.com, "Why Entrepreneurs Need To Be Good Listeners and How To Be...,"https://yourstory.com/2016/10/develop-good-listening-skills

88 Hubspot.com, "47 Uplifting Entrepreneur Quotes To Ignite Your Drive," https://blog.hubspot.com/sales/motivational-quotes-from-some-of-the-world-most-s

89 Entreprenuer.com, "Determining Your Ideal Customer,"
https://www.entrepreneur.com/article/75648

90 Marc Beaujean, Jonathan Davidson, and Stacey Madge," The Moment of Truth in Customer Service,"
https://www.mckinsey.com/business-functions/organization/our-insights/the-moment-of-truth-in-customer-service

91 Entreprenuer.com, "Go The Extra Mile If You Want To Achieve Excellence," https://www.entrepreneur.com/article/311524

92 Forbes.com, "Don't Spend 5 Times More Attracting New Customers, Nurture,"

https://www.forbes.com/sites/jiawertz/2018/09/12/dont-spend-5-times-more-attract

93 "Communication Is A Skill That You Can Learn. It's Like...," http://dvqlxo2m2q99q.cloudfront.net/000_clients/78008/file/executive-summary-.pd

94 Srhm.org, "Managing for Employee Retention," https://www.shrm.org/resourcesandtools/tools-and-samples/toolkits/pages/managingforemployeeretention.aspx

95 Gallup.com, "Employees Want A Lot More From Their Managers,"https://www.gallup.com/workplace/236570/employees-lot-managers.aspx

96 Hubspot.com, "47 Uplifting Entrepreneur Quotes To Ignite Your Drive," https://blog.hubspot.com/sales/motivational-quotes-from-some-of-the-world-most-s

97 Entrepreneur.com, "Vision: The Driver Of Entrepreneurship," https://www.entrepreneur.com/article/269757

98 "How to Create a Vision Statement for Your Business," https://www.bdc.ca/en/articles-tools/business-strategy-planning/manage-growth/pages/why-strong-vision-key-ingredient-growth-plan.aspx

99 Jack Canfield, "How to Create An Empowering Vision Board," https://www.jackcanfield.com/blog/how-to-create-an-empowering-vision-book/

100 Susan Steinbrecher, Entrepreneur.com, "The Vision Board is Your Internal GPS System to Realizing Your Dreams," https://www.entrepreneur.com/article/251023

101 Nathan Chan, "7 Interesting Things that Arianna Huffington Taught Me About Success," https://addicted2success.com/success-advice/7-interesting-things-that-arianna-huffington-taught-me-about-success/

102 Ryan Westwood, Forbes.com, "6 Things Great Entrepreneurs Don't Do That Set Them Apart,"

https://www.forbes.com/sites/ryanwestwood/2017/01/18/6-things-great-entrepreneur

103 "47 Uplifting Entrepreneur Quotes To Ignite Your Drive", https://blog.hubspot.com/sales/motivational-quotes-from-some-of-the-world-most-s

Acknowledgments

Thank you to every entrepreneur who offered insight in *The Entrepreneurial Compass*. I cherish my clients over the years who have shown the entrepreneurial spirit and the values of cooperation and teamwork.

I was lucky enough to have mentors like mindfulness teacher Betsy across many years. Together, they taught me to breathe, meditate, be mindful of my thoughts, and to use positive affirmations to help create an ideal life. They encouraged me to break through limited beliefs and claim greatness. The followings teachers have helped me significantly: Alicia Mooney, Elizabeth Wright, Dr. Jill Little, Val Cook, Bonita Shear, and Sheila Applegate. I am forever grateful to each of these teachers. Also, to the folks at The Miraval – Life in Balance who assisted me when I first needed silence to experience wellness modalities.

Entrepreneur Sharon, who appears as a case example within this book, represents many of the women I coach who are mothers, running businesses and aspiring to make time for self-care because they expend tons of energy and at times, put themselves last.

Just Richard is the name of the actual man I met in Turks and Caicos who shared pivotal advice and inspired me to write this book. I have pondered if Just Richard was a guide sent to me.

The case example of Trainwreck Jerry is based on a composite sketch of men who I have coached that long for stability, and are determined to make a positive difference through the work they perform.

I am forever grateful to the entrepreneurs and leaders at the *Lakewood Women Connecting Women* event where I spoke near Cleveland, Ohio. The conversations I had with event attendees ignited me to birth this book based on their response to my keynote speech. I am indebted to that fantastic group of people!

A special thanks to Torrey Worren for the invitation to speak at to the *Lakewood Women Honoring Women* event and for inspiring me. And to Traci Medford-Rosow, USA Today bestselling author of the books, *Inflection Point: War and Sacrifice in Corporate America*, as well as her most recent title, *UNBLINDED*. Traci connected me with her cousin Torrey, who helped become the catalyst for delivering of my keynote speech, "Ignite Your Inner Leader." I honor these women for their efforts to foster connections and sincerely appreciate their support.

I am grateful to: Chris Moebs for his exceptional talent in designing the book cover and for production layout; copy editor, Danielle Gasparro for a stellar job in editing the final version of the book; my sister Christina, who offered her vital commentary and insight as a businesswoman; and to transformational life coach, Sheila Applegate for providing the encouragement and guidance I needed to realize my highest potential in composing this book, and for the incredible support she's provided as a friend and coach over many years.

Lastly, to all the thriving entrepreneurs in the world who are creating incredible products and services, I celebrate the offering of this book with you. ♥

About the Author

Laura Ponticello is a bestselling and international award-winning author on the subject matter of personal transformation. She is a business and transformation coach, global publisher, and publicist. Laura teaches the seminars, "Unleashing Your Creativity," "Ignite the Inner Leader," and "So, You've Written a Book, What Now?" She is a bridge-builder who connects people. Laura was the Vice President of Strategic Planning for a global Fortune 500 company. Six Sigma recognized Laura for industry expertise. As a champion for personal empowerment, Laura lectures on the topics of creative entrepreneurship and the new paradigm of leadership.

You can connect with Laura to share insights, thoughts, and ideas at www.lauraponticello.com and on social media.

Other books by Laura include: Reader's Favorite winner, *Live the Life of Your Dreams, 33 Tips for Inspired Living* and International Mind, Body, Spirit award winner, *The Art of Self Transformation.*

Influencing Connections

In the spirit of supporting entrepreneurs to achieve our dreams and elevate each other to reach full potential, join the community at **www.divinephoenixbooks.com**

Learn more about seminars and speaking forums for The Creative Leader, and The New Paradigm of Leading by visiting our website and following us via social media on Facebook, Twitter, Linked In, and Instagram.

Help share the message of this book by bringing Laura to your hometown, hosting a venue, sponsoring a lecture, starting a morning or lunch meet up for entrepreneurs to support each other, and igniting conversation on social media about your journey with *The Entrepreneurial Compass.*

Made in the USA
Lexington, KY
26 April 2019